PERSONALITY
Issues in Assessment and the Projective Inventory Approach

Advances in Psychological Research in India Series

1. Perspectives on Psychology and Social Development
   U.N. Dash and **Uday Jain** (Eds.)
2. Psychology of Poverty and Disadvantages
   Ajit K. Mohanty and **Girishwar Misra** (Eds.)
3. Perspectives on Indigenous Psychology
   Girishwar Misra and **Ajit K. Mohanty**
4. Psychology of Reading: Role of Orthographic Features
   Shantilata Sahu
5. Personality: Issues in Assessment and Projective Inventory Approach
   Pratap K. Rath

About the Author

Pratap K. Rath is a reader in the Centre of Advanced Study in Psychology, Utkal University. He got his Ph.D. from the University of Exeter, U.K. He teaches research methodology, statistics, computer applications and testing. His constant endeavour to make psychology relevant to the society often finds him fighting for the rights of the exploited and the abused children, especially those having some impairment. Not a nice man to know if you belong to the opposite side or sit on the fence.

Advances in Psychological Research in India Series - 5

PERSONALITY
Issues in Assessment and the Projective Inventory Approach

By

P.K. RATH

CONCEPT PUBLISHING COMPANY PVT. LTD.
NEW DELHI-110059

ISBN: 978-81-7022-927-8

Edition 2025

Published and Printed by

Concept
Since 1974

Concept Publishing Company Pvt. Ltd.
A/15-16, Commercial Block, Mohan Garden,
New Delhi-110059 (India)
T : 91-11-41101460
E : publishing@conceptpub.com, *W*: www.conceptpub.com

Foreword

The state of psychological testing in India has been severally criticized for mindless borrowing of western tests and lack of methodological rigour in test development, use and application. The chasm between the theory of testing and practice is all the more formidable in the area of personality assessment. In this book Dr. P.K. Rath takes a critical look at the fundamental nature of psychological testing, and the psychometric requirements for the same with particular focus on personality testing. He takes a different view about the "social desirability" issue in personality assessment and proposes a tentative theory of personality testing to understand the social desirability effect. Projective-Inventory method of personality testing is analysed and projected as a more acceptable alternative in the field. This book is quite nonconventional both in terms of the style of writing as well as the arguments which question some of our fundamental assumptions about psychological testing.

The Centre of Advanced Study in Psychology, Utkal University is known for its pioneering work in the field of psychological testing and research methodology. Contributions of Professor B.N. Puhan of the CAS in Psychology at Utkal towards conceptualization and development of projective-inventory approach to personality assessment is widely acclaimed. In this book Dr. Rath takes the trends started in this direction to further heights. The CAS in Psychology is happy facilitating the publication of this volume.

This publication comes under the publication series *Advances in Psychological Research in India* taken up by the CAS in Psychology during the current phase of the UGC special assistance (1997-2002). Through the publications under this series, the Centre seeks to project the recent developments in psychological research in India. *Personality : Issues in Assessment and the Projective Inventory Approach* is a definite addition to the quality of the series and I hope that it will be appreciated by our colleagues in Psychology, researchers and students in the fields of psychological testing, personality and research methodology. There is some freshness and novelty in the arguments and points of view of the author which should affect our conventional approaches to testing and assessment.

The contribution of the UGC for publication of the series and this particular volume in gratefully acknowledged. I thank Shri Ashok Kumar Mittal of the Concept Publishing Company, New Delhi for the care in taking up publication of this work as well as other in the series.

Utkal University
Bhubaneswar
March 26, 2000

Ajit K. Mohanty
Professor and Coordinator
Centre of Advanced Study in Psychology

Preface

Personality Testing has always offered greater variety of challenges than ability testing simply because there are no right or wrong answers for the test items. Therefore, it poses greater challenges to make the testing more useful or meaningful. Of course, in India, except for a few recruitment or clinical situations, personality testing has not attained the significance it ought to have in the study of individual differences.

It has been over 20 years since the day the idea of Projective-Inventory as an approach to test personality was developed. It came from a ridiculously simple idea of marrying the two classical yet opposing approaches, (*i.e.*, the projective approach and the self-report inventory approach) to get the best of both. The product was named equally simply the Projective-Inventory. Mr. P.K. Rath worked for his Masters' degree dissertation taking this problem at that time. He later worked for his Ph.D. at Exeter in this area. This enabled him to expand the idea still further. However, barring a few M.A., M.Phil. and Doctoral level works at Utkal and a few publications, not too much have been done in the past years. Of course, the fact remains that we could not write a book on this new approach. But, in different fora of academic interactions, I have talked about the approach. That it has failed to stimulate research interest could be because the concepts involved necessitated different kinds of thinking for realizing the full impact of this approach. The flexibility it offers is hardly seen in other testing instruments. It is highly adaptable to the technological innovations like multi-media computers. In fact, its fullest reach can be explored through these gadgets as it would take out some of the tediousness of the paper-pencil tests of personality.

It is nice to have Dr P.K. Rath write about it so that this

approach can be publicized more, drawing the attention of serious researchers and critics, which will refine the process to a greater degree. We have always felt that it is the openness of ideas and thinking that enhance the quality of research. With that we can show that Indian psychologists are not just confirming hypotheses but quite capable of generating a few of their own and contributing to the general level of understanding of human behaviour.

Prof. B.N. Puhan

Acknowledgements

There has been few attempts from the Indian side to get psychologists to think about the issues that has been taken as resolved. The human mind needs constant exploration. The concepts being used by psychologists must also be challenged so that a better conceptualisation can take place. As a student of psychology, I pay tribute to this beautiful subject by acknowledging truly how far we are from what we have been dishing out as truths to others.

I am thankful to my wife, who has always asked me to get down to writing. I am grateful to Dr. A.K. Mohanty for his constant goading to meet the deadline and Dr. B.N. Puhan for the preface and the initial idea. I must sing the praise of the British system extant in 1983-86 that gave me the freedom to think, challenge and put forth in words my opposition to the well established concepts in psychology. My regards to Dr P. Kline, who bravely withstood those tumultuous years of my work under his supervision. I will be extremely grateful to the persons who care to go through this writing and send their reactions for further analysis and improvement in thought and presentation.

The quotations from *Alice in wonderland,* written by Lewis Carrol, inserted at the beginning of each chapter reflect my feelings I had some 14 years back. Funny, how the more things change, the more they appear to remain the same. My feelings remain the same, in the wonderland of academic psychology. I do not know about Alice, but I am enjoying the experience.

I salute Prof. Lumsden for his paper on test theory and his use of vulgar analogy. I thank him for writing that masterpiece which is one of its kind. I think every student of psychology should be advising to read it.

This is not meant to be a textbook on Personality. A fair bit of knowledge in that as well as in the fundamentals of testing is essential for relishing the contents.

P.K. Rath

Contents

*Foreword by **Prof. Ajit K. Mohanty*** v
*Preface by **B.N. Puhan*** vii
Acknowledgements ix

1. Introduction to a Resolution :The Projective Inventory 1
1. Methods of Testing (?) Personality *1*
1.1 The Projective Inventory Approach *5*
1.1.1 Constraints and Comparability *6*
1.1.2 A Solution of the Social Desirability Problem *7*
1.1.3 Some Reflections *8*
1.2 The Various Angles *8*

2. In Defence of Trait 10
2. Introduction *10*
2.1 The Trait versus Situation Controversy *11*
2.2 On Predicting Behaviour *13*
2.2.1 Regarding Prediction and Predictability *15*
2.2.2 The Statistics of Prediction *18*
2.2.3 The Limits of Multiple Regression *19*
2.3 Trait Position and its Defence *20*
2.3.1 Low Predictive Validity *21*
2.3.2 Lack of Consistency in Behaviour *22*
2.3.3 Cognitive Considerations *24*
2.3.4 Summing up 24
2.4 Other Alternatives 25
2.5 Preliminary Analysis of Some Contentions *29*
2.5.1 The Theory of Opposing Forces *30*

2.5.2 Socialization and Growth of Traits *32*
2.5.3 The Process of Social Reinforcement *34*
2.5.4 Applying Theory to Oneself *35*
2.5.5 About the Fixity of Traits *36*
2.5.6 On Consistency *38*
2.6 The Contribution of PI Approach *41*
2.6.1 The Computation of Dynamism Indices *42*
2.7 The Kernel of Truth *44*

3 The Social Desirability Effect 46
3. The Initial Idea *46*
3.1 The Discovery *47*
3.2 SD in Projection Tests *51*
3.3 The Fight for Survival *52*
3.3.1 Technological Advancement and Anti-SD Warfare *57*
3.4 How to Stop "Faking"? *58*
3.5 On Establishing Rapport *59*
3.6 On Asking Silly Questions *61*
3.7 SD and Reality *62*
3.8 Meehl's Faking and Jourard's Confession *65*
3.9 Do People Behave in a Socially Desirable way? *68*
3.10 What is Social about Social Desirability *68*
3.11 Law of Parsimony and the SD *71*
3.12 In a Nutshell *73*

4 On Reliability and Validity of Tests 75
4. Introduction *75*
4.1 The Concept *77*
4.1.1 Some Practical Limitations *78*
4.1.2 Error of Measurement (judgment ?) *80*
4.1.3 Some Theoretical Issues *82*
4.1.3.1 The Error Component of True Score *83*
4.1.4 Why Reliability ? *85*
4.1.5 Consistency of Persons or Reliability of Tests? *86*
4.2 The Formulation *88*
4.2.1 Face Validity *89*

4.2.2 Content Validity *89*
4.2.3 The Multitrait-Multimethod Approach *90*
4.2.4 Construct Validity *92*
4.2.4.1 Some Objections *94*
4.3 So How Do We Develop a Test ? *95*
4.4 What Happens Then ? *97*
4.5 Related Afterthought *98*

5. Test of the Pudding 100
5. Putting the PI Idea to Test *100*
5.1 The PIAPEN *101*
5.2 The Statements and Their Keying *102*
5.2.1 A Case for Multiple Keying *103*
5.2.2 The Item Format *105*
5.3 The Rationale and the Objectives *106*
5.3.1 A Pilot Study *108*
5.3.2 The Sample and Testing *108*
5.3.3 Data Analysis *109*
5.4 The Rationale the Objectives *110*
5.4.1 The Sample *111*
5.4.2 Testing *111*
5.4.3 Data Analysis *113*
5.4.3.1 Scoring *113*
5.4.3.2 On Using Factor Analysis *113*
5.4.3.3 The Preliminary Analysis *115*
5.4.3.4 Looking Back *116*
5.3.4.5 Final Analysis *118*

6. Towards a Better Future 120
6. At the End of the Day *120*
6.1 About Item Selection and Keying *124*
6.2 Bouquets and Brickbats *131*
6.3 Epilogue *132*

Appendices

Introduction to Appendices 135
A. The Indian Version of PIAPEN : The Initial Test 136
B. The Initial Statements 144
C. Scoring Key of the Indian Version of PIAPEN 155

Bibliography 156
Index 167

"Begin at the beginning", the King said, very gravely, "and go on till you come to the end: then stop."

One

Introduction to a Resolution: The Projective Inventory

1. Methods of Testing (?) Personality

I could just do that, I mean, follow the King's advice. But unfortunately this topic has too many beginnings and has no end (to madness) in sight. If I have to begin at the beginning. I would have to begin many times and, worse still, I would not be able to stop at the end as I would have come to another beginning. I would, therefore, start somewhere in the middle and leave the end to the readers.

While everybody wants to be able to predict the future behaviour of the individual, we, the psychologists, feel we are officially responsible. But since it is somewhat like test cricket (no official world champions and there is money to be made.) we get pushed and shoved by soothsayers, astrologers, palmists, numerologists, graphologists and what-not-logists while trying to get people's attention and their money. So, we try to show the world that our scientific predictions are based on what the person has been doing with his/her life (often behind everybody's back and sometime his/her own). Of course, we are not quite sure how to name the process (such as testing, assessment, evaluation and measurement, etc.) but that has not deterred us from producing tests like our lives depended on them. And in the process, we have been getting at each other's academic throat sometimes. But these are all very understandable.

The methods of testing are like political parties in India, which try to retain their identity in spite of the followers freely changing their allegiance and the manifestoes they put up looking incrediably similar. Somehow, among the multitudes of methods, projective techniques and the inventory method have managed to dominate the arena in relative exclusion of the other. In the cutthroat world of academic research, there are many more adherents and exponents of the two methods who are opposed to the other method than are those who accept the fact that the gap between them can be bridged (Buros, 1959, 1965, 1972, 1978; Coloney *et al.* 1988, 1989, 1994, 1995)..

Projective methods, with their esoteric application, found support mostly in the clinical area. This is the area, which faces the crises of human personality at its worst point. The insistence is, therefore, more on understanding an individual facing his own idiosyncratic problems than on comparing his performance with that of a group to which he belongs. The rules are accordingly flexible and permit alternative interpretations. Though every clinician felt that his conception was true, the sheer lack of interpretive agreement signifies that the complexity of human personality is far from being unraveled. Projective techniques utilize mostly unstructured tasks, which permit a large variety of responses to be elicited in a testing situation. In this regard, Anastasi (1976) stated, "The underlying hypothesis is that the way in which the individual perceives and interprets the test materials will serve as a sort of screen on which the respondent projects his characteristic thought processes, needs, anxieties, conflicts" (p. 558-559). The projective technique users apparently believe in unconscious motivation and subjectivity of responses yielded. There have been various attempts to standardize the scoring and to smarten up the appearance from the occult to the physical. Still the projective techniques require more interpretation that are based more on the individual's point of view than on readily agreed upon principles as is true of the inventories.

The inventories consist of questions or statements regarding a person's feelings, perception, cognition etc. The logical base of such an approach is the fact that a person lives with himself much longer than he ever does with anybody else. So the person has more access to the relevant information about himself than anybody else does. Therefore, the best way of knowing about a person is to ask him. It needs to be emphasized that the proof of this contention is as elusive as the proof of the projective hypothesis. Somehow, it is only when projective techniques are described, the term "hypothesis" conspicuously crops up. Its absence in the writings on inventories, by default, implies that what the inventories reveal constitute a greater part of reality than what they can not reveal. Though the logic is understandable, it is not, in any way, proved on *a priori* grounds.

This roughly being the main difference between the two approaches, fine grain analyses done by various textbooks reveal a dozen more differences. To these highly technical analyses, one can add Kelly's (1955) observation. "When the subject is asked to guess what the examiner is thinking, we call it an objective test: When the examiner tries to guess what the subject is thinking, we call it a projective device" (P. 332). Statements like this, apart from the fun they provide, have contributed substantially in keeping the two approaches apart.

One could very well discern another trend in their development. Inventories, with all the trappings of a scientific method, gained quick acceptance in the academic sphere. Projective methods found acceptance in the clinical area. Both the methods have grown in complete insulation from the findings in the other area. While psychometricians lament the lack of any acceptable demonstration of reliability and validity the clinicians lament the superficiality of the inventory approach. Each of the approaches has some attractive features for the end-users' purposes not offered by the other. In many cases, this double approach-avoidance conflict in the choice of personality tests led psychologists to look for alternatives. It is no wonder that the alternatives mentioned below came up with completely different techniques. There is nothing wrong with such endeavors except that they never gave the traditional methods a chance for modification — a fresh lease of life.

Puhan (1982) critically evaluated the various approaches to personality measurements using the traditional concepts of reliability and validity. He analyzed, on the strength of empirical evidence put forth, that the projective tests suffer from low reliability and validity and inventories from low validity. A close analysis of various other attempts at providing the alternatives such as, the Grid approach (Bannister & Bott, 1973), the Picture-Association Test (Rozenzweig, 1945), the Conflict-Resolution approach (Kohlberg, 1963; 1964; 1969), and the Projectometry approach (Sandven, 1975) revealed that they have met with limited success. The author has some reservations about the critique, because most of the criticisms centered around the psychometric concepts of reliability and validity, which have been analyzed to be not-so-infallible benchmarks of test efficacy later in this writing.

Apart from these paper and pencil tests, there have been claims for the use of the so-called situational tests which would apparently provide an unadulterated version of behaviour from which the disciplined mind of a researcher can make an objective abstraction for analyses. Such abstraction would be superior to the rather naive abstraction of the respondent. Apart from the fallacious nature of the contention, the sheer number of factors like time, expense, behavioural taxonomy, the problems of time and event sampling, reactivity etc. have been so forbidding that, since the epic efforts of Hartshorne & May (1928; 1929), not many notable studies have been conducted using these so-called realistic situational tests. Still, it must be accepted that those studies provided valuable insight into the possibility of situational tests, which would test cross-situational consistency of behaviour. Some of the alternative tests like the Picture-Frustration Test and the Conflict-Resolution Test etc. have tried to incorporate some situational relevance into the testing environment. Though the inventories have not changed very much, it must be admitted that the role of context as determining behaviour in comparison with traits is being given increasing recognition.

Puhan & Rath (1981) argued that the projective tests were not susceptible to social desirability effect because the responses yielded were numerous and ambiguous. But their administration and scoring were not as efficient because of the subjectivity involved. The apparent ease with which inventories could be administered was deemed to be an attractive aspect as well. But those two methods were so much opposed to each other that one almost resigned oneself to the inevitability of choosing between an unreliable approach and an invalid one.

Then followed the scandalous suggestion, more implied than stated, of a possible marriage between the two approaches to produce a hybrid which would have their best features. In that crossbreeding (mis?)adventure, one was quite likely to come up with a product that retained all the limitations of the parents. But then what is research without a fair dose of optimism? Fortified with that optimism, the idea was carefully nurtured and the Projective Inventory approach took shape.

1.1 The Projective Inventory Approach

Puhan & Rath (1981) found the bridge and tried a simple solution in the Projective Inventory (henceforth referred to as the PI) approach. There was no attempt to coin one's own neologism (there are too many of them littering the highway of psychological research) to describe the method. The primacy of projective approach in the naming merely reflected the convenience and did not show its relative importance *vis-a-vis* the inventory approach. It must be emphasized that the PI does not refer to any single test. It is a method, which provides the guidelines for developing different tests. In order to develop a test under the PI approach the two aspects should be given equal importance. The first one should contain, as far as possible, descriptions of human interaction in real life situations, which the respondent could project into. The second aspect should help in eliciting the relevant response for analysis via the inventory-like statements. This would provide a good blend for individual's feeling of freedom and the tester's need to access the trait without much contrivance.

1.1.1 Constraints and Comparability

No approach can be without constraints however comprehensive its scope happens to be. There are always some constraints involved even in the so-called relatively freer projective methods: The Thematic Apperception Test (Murray *et al.*, 1938) uses pictures of human beings as its constraint whereas the InkBlot Test (Rorschach, 1945) uses colour and form as its constraints. The constraints, however, are not very restrictive in comparison with the inventory statements. From a normative research point of view, the argument against less constraint is that the responses yielded refer to less comparable situations than is the case with the inventory approach. Moreover, it was wrongly implied that because inventories permit only a very limited number of response categories they provide an objective measure of the trait. The statements may seem to be very straightforward but each respondent makes his/her own idiosyncratic judgment about the implication of the statements. The fact that we use our own personal experiences and attitudes to make sense of the concepts that we use makes it clear that there is a lot of subjectivity involved in the responses which the questions/ statements yield. For example, when faced with a question like "Do you believe in the institution of marriage?" the respondents are hardly likely to think of some abstract, idealized concept of marriage that we all reportedly seem to share. They are more likely to refer to their own or shared experiences or other credible information sources. In that sense, neither the situation they are referring to is comparable nor the inference that can be drawn is unequivocal. Words and sentences can be more susceptible to the vagaries of cognition than are pictures in a psychological sense. If the stimulus situations one refers to are similar then the various reactions they elicit can be compared meaningfully in a normative sense. Therefore, in the first part of development of a test in the PI approach, narrations depicting various situations are used. In the second part, instead of allowing the respondent complete freedom, inventory-like statements regarding the situation described or the characters contained therein are given. This approach provides a kind of situational test equivalent in paper-and-pencil test form with attendant ease of administration and removing some financial and a few ethical constraints.

1.1.2 A Solution of the Social Desirability Problem

The idea of developing tests through the PI approach seemed incredibly simple and effective. It was analyzed that since the projective techniques utilize ambiguous stimuli, they are less susceptible to social desirability effect. Moreover, the statements in inventories always directly refer to the person concerned who justifiably feel as being under a microscope. This feeling, in a way, pushes the person into giving socially desirable response in the tests. PI technique utilizes a kind of evaluative statement arguably about some situation or other persons not obviously related to the person being evaluated. Thus it was projected to be well equipped to tackle the problem of social desirability. Such was the faith (mostly misplaced) that Puhan and Rath decided to develop a test of honesty (a trait having high social desirability) using the PI approach. This, as would be expected under the circumstances, met with limited success. There was a problem in the validity criterion as there was opposition to provide the ratings. There was no method of otherwise testing the efficacy of such a venture with adults when the raters' cooperation was not easily forthcoming.

But, in the euphoria that followed this prototype testing, the limited nature of the success was found acceptable. Later attempts at developing tests through the PI method has met with greater success. Puhan's report in the Indian Council for Social Science Research (ICSSR) Publication mentions that the tests have shown considerable convergent validity and less discriminant validity using the Multitrait-Multimethod approach. Some studies have come up with evidence to show the resistance of such tests against social desirability effect (Puhan & Roy, 1985; Patnaik, 1985).

1.1.3 Some Reflections

It needs to be pointed out that the author was very skeptical about projection as a general process as well as the efficacy of stories (as in the PI tests) to elicit the required responses. There had not been any significant demonstration of the uses of the PI technique. There was no theoretical base for such a development. It was more like wishful thinking (though admittedly on integrative lines) combined with a platonic conception of the testing process (in comparison with the other techniques that were offered as alternatives). There have not been many relevant studies to demonstrate how far this approach has been able to achieve what it purported to achieve in the beginning, *i.e.*, to make the tests less susceptible against social desirability effect than the inventories while providing the relevant trait information of comparable value. However, as the study progressed, developments in related areas have shed new light on the problem. Those developments that led to rethinking about fundamental issues related to testing are briefly described below.

1.2 The Various Angles

There have been three apparently unrelated areas that have been undergoing upheavals either as reported in the research articles or as revealed through critical analysis. Ultimately all branches of psychology must converge to solve the problem of measurement, prediction and understanding of human behaviour. The greater the apparent unrelatedness of the areas, the worse becomes the chance of achieving integration. Therefore, the attempt has been to integrate, as far as possible, the various areas that are deemed to be significantly contributing to the main effort.

The relevant areas were: (1) the trait versus situation controversy, (2) the apparent pervasiveness and virulence of the social desirability effect, and (3) the efficacy of the psychometric monoliths like reliability and validity. The first relevant problem area was the conceptualization of the traits. The traits are concepts that stood for consistency in the midst of rampant behavioural inconsistency across situations. The trait concept had functioned as the hope that served to guide research in psychometry even in the face of limited success. Then comes the analysis of the social desirability effect. It referred to the idea of a respondent not responding as per his/her true feelings but in accordance with what he/she felt to be socially desirable. Of course, the process is deemed to be unconscious and therefore, less amenable to manipulation. Finally, the way the tests were evaluated for their efficacy also came under scrutiny. While reliability referred to the consistency of scores across time and space, validity sought to locate the extent to which a test measured what it purported to measure. These three apparently unrelated areas have shed considerable light on the way a reconceptualization of personality and its assessment has taken place, hopefully for the better. There are obvious repetitions, as is unavoidable in an attempt to integrate the findings in the related areas. It has served to strengthen the PI approach.

The idea of a PI method was born and brought up in a protected environment. Even though the world around was falling apart, Puhan & Rath went on following the traditional ways. (But it must be admitted that they were just two of the crowd that followed the tradition). On one side, the very concept of trait was under threat of losing its identity in the trait versus situation controversy. On the other side, all our valiant efforts to kill the archenemy of testing movement, the social desirability effect, proved ineffective. On another side the solid pillars of the psychometric theorization such as the concepts of reliability and validity, had come under attack. And this time the damage was done by some of the insiders (led by Lumsden). The newborn (the PI approach) has grown very quickly and has received its baptism under fire coming from all the directions. In view of that wisdom, old views were changed and old problems have been tackled in a clearer perspective.

The following chapters describe the efforts in the order it is described in the previous paragraph. Such ordering is a matter of descriptive convenience rather than of importance. The problems and controversies involved are critically analyzed and the performance of the PI approach is evaluated.

"That is a great deal to make one word mean", Alice said in a thoughtful tone.

Two

In Defence of Trait

2. Introduction

Though inventories have measured traits for a long time, the origin of traits has always been controversial. While a few called them reified factors (Tryon, 1979), Eysenck (1953a) hypothesized bio-genetically determined behavioural dispositions. Hogan *et. al.* (1977) argued that they were merely common or shared descriptors. But psychometricians have traditionally ignored the theory of origin and gone on the professional's way of "You name it, we measure it". Initially, the concept of trait was created to enable the psychometricians to abstract a consistency from the reported or observed behaviour. This was supposed to be used to predict similar kinds of behaviour shown subsequently. However, once the so-called predictive validity was established, psychometricians did not really bother to predict any single behaviour. So the hypothesis of consistency of behaviour, by definition, was never tested and was simply assumed to be true! It allowed the tests measuring the traits to have some kind of extra-behavioural connotation that was never really there. This also helped the psychometricians in conveniently ignoring the social psychologists who have been vociferously criticizing the lack of situational relevance in testing. But now the controversy centres around the utility of the traditional concept of trait for understanding and explaining non-existent consistency of behaviour. Psychometricians have curiously been very wary of social psychologists (situationists), their traditional rivals, in the competition to explain behaviour. Lest it be construed that the author is another wolf (social psychologist) in sheep's (psychometrician's) clothing, it must be mentioned that interrelated disciplines can grow in relative isolation only for so long. It is time we realized that some of the research going on in the adjacent areas can really clarify a few points and can even cure some of the chronic ailments that we, the psychometricians, seem to be having.

2.1 The Trait versus Situation Controversy

The mention of trait versus situation debate as a raging controversy will be a real understatement or rather a misleading statement. It is a chaos, as can be witnessed for a starter in Magnusson & Endler (1977). There is an abundance of wanton research articles in various journals for those who are more inclined towards getting a stronger flavour of the controversy. In any case, books like that are attempts to bring some semblance of order into the debate but merely manage to muddle the issues. If only a set of questions were put to every author, some kind of comparison would be possible. Unfortunately, the field has turned out to be a free-for-all intellectual fracas where everybody joins in for the pleasure of the fray. (or is it a sample of the thing we hear about called "the publish or perish syndrome?")

Apparently, Mischel (1968) started it all, digging into the evidence and coming up with the suggestion of a 'personality coefficient' of .3 in trying to explain behaviour. He meant that the trait concept could explain only about 10 percent of the variance in the behaviour being studied. Situationists being the traditional rivals of trait position, Mischel was immediately identified as belonging to the enemy camp (situationists) and some trait theorists attacked him. Mischel (1973; 1977; 1979; 1982) has been shouting hoarsely since then that he meant something different such as a cognitive replacement of the dominantly affective and social nature of the traits. But the fun had started and so good is the attraction of the controversies in the academic world, lacking in any creative stimulation (Fiske, 1978), that even after nearly two decades there seems to be little abatement excepting for the general lethargy.

A little digression towards a theory of controversy will help in appreciating the perspectives and deja vus (Bem's favourite) involved. Meehl (1978), in a thought provoking article deplored the slow progress of soft psychology while also showing why (roughly 20 solid reasons) psychology could not proceed at a faster speed. It is this slow progress which, throughout the ages, has incensed some psychologists namely Watson, Mischel and others into stirring up controversies. It is mostly because we, the psychologists, in our unholy haste of becoming scientists have tried to ape the methods (somewhat akin to the logic of becoming a doctor by donning a stethoscope) forgetting the philosophical issues that we seem to be having bouts of the same controversy at various intervals as recorded in various sources (Bem & Allen, 1974; Bem, 1983a). It needs to be mentioned that it is not true only of the soft areas (meaning social, clinical psychology etc.) but also of the hard areas (*e.g.*, animal psychology). Mackintosh (1974) is a voluminous witness to the fads and fictions in animal psychology. The same author mentioned (1983) that derided by cognitive psychologists, ethologists, and neuroscientists for different reasons, animal psychology has been freed of its pretensions as the golden road to a science of human behaviour. But it is stronger for that and is to be viewed as a branch of study in its own right. (It is only to be hoped that the beleaguered psychometricians do not follow in the steps and proclaim that a study of human test-taking behaviour is a discipline in its own right). In any case, it has been almost repeatedly shown that the controversies have never been resolved. They merely fade away as research interest in the area wanes and the futility of any extreme viewpoint in a complex subject is realized. That does not mean that any new thinking of an old problem should be received with condescension or apprehension. Not every disgruntled psychologist is a potential Watson, promising a lot and fading away without trace. A controversy always requires a moderator who could make the dialogue or rather the multilogues intelligible as clarifying a problem and providing potential answers.

Since it is hoped that psychometricians would not demand that traits be studied on their own, the trait, however inferred, must ultimately be linked to some measurable phenomena, mostly behavioural. Having said that, it must be admitted that there are some very obvious constraints on the magnitude of the predictive efficiency of every reported or conceivable measuring instrument. Traits are abstracted by various degree of remoteness from observed behaviour. Mostly, they function as a global description of a generalized tendency to show a logically consistent (at least from the test developer's point of view) pattern of interrelated behaviours. It must be emphasized that traits were not suited to predict a single behaviour. And yet, as soon as Mischel (1968) stated the obvious fact of a predictive limit of .30 correlation, trait supporters not only misunderstood his contention, but also tried to tackle the criticism by refurbishing the image of trait, which it was never suited to have. In this context it is worth analyzing the adventure of predicting behaviour as taking place in psychology.

2.2 *On Predicting Behaviour*

After Watson's (1913) attempt to wish the Organism away in the rather crudely stated mathematical expression B = F(S, O) where B is any Behaviour, S is Stimulus situation, and O is the responding Organism) failed, psychologists have rather grudgingly accepted that the organism has a role to play in predicting behaviour. And it was not the inconceivable, unfathomable organismic factors that were accepted. A highly structured trait score as the main determinant of behaviour replaced a highly structured description of situational variables. All we needed to add to this basic illusion of predictability was the formulation of the revered multiple regression with its awe-inspiring beta weights.

Kline (1983) mentions, "The basic equation states that any act or behaviour of an individual can be predicted from the linear addition of his scores on the major factors of ability, temperament dynamics and states, together with some measures of the environmental stimulus, all weighted in accordance with their importance for the criterion behaviour.

The specification equation :

$$a_{iJ} = b_{Ji} F_{ii} + b_{J2} F_{2i} \ldots + b_{JN} F_{Ni}$$

Where a, the action in situation J for individual i, is best estimated by the status of i on Factors F_i to F_N and by the weights b_J on the factors of the situation". (P.105).

The equation needs close observation. There are many in psychology who dislike the complexity of human behaviour being reduced to mathematical equations. Some are skeptical even when they do not resent mathematics. However, the skepticism would surely perish, if not by the sheer force of optimism that exudes from the equation then from the sheer weight of beta weights. Usually one sees an error term in prediction equation mostly symbolized by a lower case e in proportion to the importance attached to it. But, in this equation of Kline no such weaknesses can be discerned. As a continuation of his discussion, Kline mentions, "The test of the model, as we have indicated, is powerful and simple. If the model were perfect, totally without error, our correlation would be 1. The further they depart from 1 and approach zero, the worse the model. The few tests of the model that exist demonstrate that correlations around 0.3 can be obtained. Whether this result be due to the problem of models per se (e.g., its additivity and linearity), to the choice of variables, to inefficient measures, to problem of the criterion measure or to any or all of these is not yet clear." (p. 106). Kline must have echoed the sentiments of many trait psychologists whose fond hope is that they were able to predict the behaviour of human beings as precisely as Physics does the behaviour of a rocket sent to the moon. Noble though the thoughts are, pointing out some of the pitfalls of such reasoning can stop the acute frustration that usually follows an unduly high expectation.

2.2.1 Regarding Prediction and Predictability

The philosophical and psychological considerations involved in predictability are discussed here first. It is very difficult to compromise the humanists' (that description would fit quite a few trait psychologists in their social lives) ideal of democracy, freedom, individuality with the sciences' ideal of prediction and understanding. Even the great Einstein once remarked that it was incomprehensible that the world would be comprehensible. He should know because he was dealing with intangible entities. And we psychologists should know still better because we have the greatest complexity in human behaviour to deal with. That complexity is an integral part of human interaction even in the simplest of conditions. Rapaport (1962), in the context of predicting the other person's behaviour in two-person guessing game stated, "It is easy to conclude that the best pattern is no pattern. The best way to ensure this is to abdicate your role as decision-maker and let chance decide for you. Coin tossing as a guide to strategy is in this case not an act of desperation but a rational policy" (P.118). This seems to be the case where persons have freedom of choice even though the number of so-called relevant variables seem to be smaller than the number involved in social situation in every day life.

The position, from the viewpoint of the scientists in psychology, seems much better in the experimental and clinical contexts. We aim to predict the behaviour of the individual who is either seeking help or has agreed to cooperate. So the behaviour becomes predictable from a position of authority. There might also be a strong demand characteristic of the situation which acts as a self-fulfilling prophecy. In any case, we do see some predictability in such circumstances. These are reflective of the power some social institutions can and do have over our lives. But the indomitable independent spirit of human beings which seems to be brought out even in most trying situation shows that life is not that predictable. One must, therefore, differentiate between predictability as inferred from previous behaviour and the misleading idea of inevitability of such regimentation. Individuals may become predictable because of their habitual mode of responding, but that, in no way, should imply that such habits somehow force the individuals to do something without they wanting to do it. While there are exceptions to the rule, it cannot be said that such predictability characterizes most of our social situation. Psychologists can only expect a tiny bit of predictability by discerning a trend in the demonstrated or reported behaviour, and that is what they mostly get. Like astrologers and soothsayers, we have our fond strategies of locating those guiding indices. But it is not to be achieved in an environment where one's ability to bluff against another's is tested. Most of the testing situation turns out to be like that if one has a sensible look at the questions being asked by the inventories. We are to blame for the situation we have created. That has left us facing the Minsk-Pinsk dilemma (Bell, 1972) described below:

Two men are standing in a railroad station. The first asks, "Where are you going ?" "To Minsk", the other replies, "to buy some cotton goods". "Huh", snorts the first, "you are telling me you are going to Minsk to buy some cotton goods to make me think you are going to Pinsk to buy some woolen goods, but I know you are going to Minsk to buy some cotton goods; so why do you tell me lies?" (p. 7). (The discussion in the chapter on social desirability highlights the problem of psychologists trying to outsmart the test-takers and facing the same dilemma without realizing it).

Scheibe (1979) after a discussion on the predictability of behaviour and the position of psychology *vis-a-vis* science and history concluded, "Psychology is located just along the fault line between the sciences and the humanities. The tension between these areas is persistent and sometime very intense. But our mission is one of synthesis. It is to be hoped that psychology will retain the internal integrity necessary to do the mediating task" (p. 159). Unfortunately, psychology has been leaning too far toward science to do the mediation properly. And there has been two many earthquakes along the fault lines that has not helped psychology any further in understanding human behaviour.

For many, being scientific has mostly meant a rigorous use of statistics. Statisticians are those curious bunch in psychology whose esoteric mathematical formulations are kept in high regard except possibly by some recalcitrant psychometricians who feel that behind the symbols there may not be anything of psychological substance. They usually deal with numbers. And yet, they do take time off to dabble with philosophy and, when it occurs, it is worth referring to them. Cronbach (1975) mentioned: "Scientific discipline is what we uniquely add to the time-honoured ways of studying man. Too narrow an identification with science, however, has fixed our eyes upon an inappropriate goal. The goal of our work is not to amass generalizations atop which a theoretical tower can some day be erected. The special task of the social scientist in each generation is to pin down the contemporary facts. Beyond that, he shares with the humanistic scholar and the artist in the effort to gain insight into contemporary relationship and to realign the culture's view of man in present realities. To know man as he is, is no mean aspiration" (P. 126).

The quotation carries no extraordinary hopes for a predictive science of human behaviour. The implication is that mathematical models would somehow continue to be imperfect models of behaviour for a long time and only limited success is to be expected. In this context Dawes (1979), another hardheaded statistician said : "Intellectually, I find it somewhat remarkable that we are able to predict even 10% of the variance". That was stated while arguing in support of the use of multiple regression as opposed to the use of clinical judgement for making decisions. The above statements do not exactly encourage the delusion of psychology being in need of, now or in near foreseeable future, being an exact science with near perfect prediction. That is not to deny that there are some discernible consistencies of behaviour in human life. People use habitual mode of responding to cut down the demand on their adaptive ability. Such habits mostly are determined by the idiosyncratic mode of perception, thinking, feeling and reacting. Prediction depending on the discernibility of such modes, can be made albeit in a limited way.

2.2.2 The Statistics of Prediction

To be consistent with the philosophical stand taken, Kline's multiple regression model would be required to accept a rather enlarged E (for Error) in the equation. Along with that, a change in the perspective would not only save psychometricians' grace but also give Mischel a good run for his money. Kline argued in favour of the model by citing its maximum efficiency, *i.e.,* the case that would yield a correlation of 1 with the criterion. From those dizzy heights a step down to the magnitude of .3 (mostly) to .5 (rarely) correlations seems like an anti-climax. Moreover, in statistical terms the argument seems to suggest that the efficiency of the prediction model be tested for significance against perfect correlation. It is not difficult to see that Kline's model will not survive such a test. It can be pointed out that the efficiency of a model used for prediction should not be assessed relative to its maximum efficiency but in relation to what happens when that model is absent. A typical null hypothesis would suggest that there is no correlation between the predictors and the criterion. From that a .3 correlation which occurs with such regularity will work out to be highly significant as far as furthering knowledge is concerned. This argument would make Rorer and Widiger (1983) unhappy though. They contended, "When a precise hypothesis is compared with an imprecise alternative, conventional procedures often lead to erroneous conclusions, such as rejecting the null hypothesis when its likelihood is greater than that of the alternative" (p. 443). Though one can easily argue that (unfortunately), that is the way data are analyzed in psychological research, a better argument is that the multiple regression happens to be the only viable model for contention. It is the only model so far which persons having no pretension of clinical expertise or professional acumen of a particular area can use. We simply do not have any other alternative against which the efficiency of regression model can be tested.

2.2.3 The Limits of Multiple Regression

Even while supporting the model it is advisable to be aware of its limitations which helps in more efficacious use especially when such limitations turn out to be rather severe sometimes. First of all, the beta weights are notoriously unstable, fluctuating wildly from sample to sample. It is more so in the sphere of personality research. Of course, there are enough plausible excuses (confounding variables) to sustain the illusion of beta weight invariability in the population. But soon wisdom gained after repeated failures makes one accept the so-called improper linear models (non-optimal, mostly unit beta weights). These adaptations are perfectly logical and usable for psychology's immediate requirements, the fact that each variable is given equal importance makes one doubt the ultimate utility of such an approach. Secondly, another fact, very curiously overlooked in psychology, is that data analyses mostly deal with the variances and covariances of scores and that there is a clear relationship between multiple correlation and analysis of variance (Cohen 1968; 1978). Though, for long, the analysis of variance has taken psychological research for a ride, only in the 70's was it realized that it cannot be a crucible for contending theories (Bowers, 1973; Meehl, 1978). One can easily devise his own experiments to show that the variables advocated by him explain the largest variance than the contending ones. Multiple regression suffers from comparable disadvantages. One can get similar multiple correlations with the criterion using different sets of predictors, especially when the magnitude of the correlation yielded is so low. Barring the fact that some predictors look and sound more scientific than others, there is no *a priori* ground or tests of significance to prove that they are, in fact, better than the others.

When the predictors are proper orthogonal factors without any interaction, the number of expressions in the regression equation might stay manageably small. But usually the predictors are some observed behaviour like an obtained score on a test etc. whose orthogonality with other test scores are sought to be replaced by the orthogonality of factor scores. But the idea of orthogonal factors is not universally accepted as fitting explanations of correlations in psychological data. So one would not be wrong to suggest that there is always some amount of correlation between psychological factors as derived by the factor analytic processes. Moreover, there seems to be rapid discovery of various moderator and suppressor variables even when a few salient factors are used for prediction. Comparably, it can be mentioned that an analysis of variance using even only three factors quickly becomes unwieldy and poses considerable difficulty for the comprehension of higher order interaction effects. Pundits advise a strong theoretical basis for predicting such interaction as well as understanding the process. Cohen has already been referenced as demonstrating the clear relationship between analysis of variance and multiple regression. It is not very difficult to infer that multiple regression will not go very far with the rather wishful N number of factors. This discussion clarifies that multiple regression as a model is not the answer to attacks on trait concept. But it is a plausible defense against the criticism of inefficiency accruing from the repeated demonstration low correlation with the criterion as shown in the Mischel (1968).

2.3 Trait Position and its Defence

Before the trait position is defended, one must have a clear notion of what the attacks were all about. It might seem like stating the obvious but even a cursory glance at the literature will reveal that this is not always adhered to. Poor Mischel (1968) is atoning for the sin of attacking the sentiments of trait psychologists, proclaiming a .3 limit for the personality coefficient at a time when the trait supporters themselves must have been feeling that they have not progressed very far. It has served to unite the many factions in the trait camp who are bent on denying all evidences which provide the opportunity for a long overdue reconsideration. Mischel has been trying to clarify his contention intermittently (1973; 1979; 1982; 1983) since then. But the first impression he gave to others (being a situationist and all that) is almost indelible (*e.g.*, Kline, 1983; Rorer and Widiger, 1983). However, it is only fair that he is given a fair hearing.

Mischel, by his theorization, is not a situationist. When he spoke about the limits of traits as predictors he wanted the traits to be replaced for the following reasons, such as: (1) low predictive validity, (2) lack of demonstrated consistency of behaviour broadly identified as trait-like, and (3) too much of insistence on the affective tone and genetic determinism to the negligence of cognitive considerations. These points are dealt with separately in the following paragraphs.

2.3.1 Low Predictive Validity

The previous discussion of the regression model has already pointed out that a low predictive correlation does not imply that if the concept of trait were thrown out of the equation then the predictive ability would rise suddenly. There is a lot of variance (conveniently identified as error) still left to be explained. The alternatives could easily be developed without first having to run down the traits as predictors. But it must be admitted that that is how the research in academic psychology runs. In statistical terms, if Mischel is desperately in need of getting rid of traits then he has to demonstrate a substantial correlation with the criterion using the alternative. Given the state of theorization, convention and measurement in psychology, such an eventuality does not seem very likely. Even if such an outcome takes place, a trait, the cognitive alternative and their combination may prove to be better predictors than the cognitive alternative alone.

2.3.2 Lack of Consistency in Behaviour

The consistency of trait indicative behaviour has been the point of continuing debate (Bem & Allen, 1974; Magnusson & Endler, 1977; Epstein, 1979; Mischel & Peake, 1982; Bem, 1983; Funder, 1983; Mischel & Peake, 1983; Epstein, 1983). The term consistency has two aspects: temporal and cross-situational. Goldberg (1972) remarked that confusion on that issue has led to an 'enormous amount of poppycock' being published. To be fair, the poppycock also includes the one by Goldberg who contended that while persons do fluctuate over situations the rank order positions of the persons remains invariant. Kline (1983) is very much inclined towards such a view. Analogous to a pecking order in the birds and animals, such a view takes a rather low view of the human beings and a high view of their traits. Briefly speaking, it theorizes that human beings do fluctuate across situations, but since others involved in the situations also fluctuate in the expected direction faithfully like some obsequious courtiers the relative position (the pecking order) remains unchanged. This futility of such a position is discussed later in the section on reconceptualization.

Bem & Allen (1974) answered the question of consistency by contending that some people are more consistent than others are. They argued that the trait theorists' conception of what the underlying link between the reportedly consistent behaviour was might not coincide with what the individual himself felt about it. That would yield apparent inconsistency when measured from the trait theorist's point of view. So the inconsistency is not because there is no consistency but because the trait theorists are looking at wrong places for it. This simple solution seems scandalously akin to one given by the PI approach. In fact, the data showed that the persons who are deemed to be consistent by their near and dear ones are the persons who rate themselves as consistent on that dimension. This study has two important implications for the PI approach. The first one is that there was an attempt to measure the variation of a trait. Secondly, it gave importance to the discovery of consistencies from the obvious inconsistencies as distinct from the traditional way of forcing consistency through item analysis. Very much like other traits they simply asked their subjects about how consistent they were on a particular trait. This way of leaving everything to the respondents may over-burden their adaptive and self-awareness abilities. The strategy and the test used, therefore, in the PI approach is quite different.

Epstein (1979) showed that consistency of persons could not be demonstrated across each and every individual segment of the manifestation of trait indicative behaviour. Consistency of behaviour referred to and made better sense when an average pattern of behaviour was taken into consideration. However, that study did not distinguish between temporal consistency and the cross-situational consistency, which had been the bone of contention.

Mischel & Peake (1982), in a fine grain analysis of behaviour of individuals reported to be consistent, showed that even such individuals show no cross-situational consistency. But they found temporal consistency very clearly. They tried to explain the growing conviction of laypersons and trait theorists alike that human beings do behave consistently (as was originally stated by Bem and Allen) by stating that people respond consistently to or in the presence of the rater creating the illusion of consistency. Though the situation apparently changes, the position of authority (the presence of someone) could determine a consistency that would not otherwise occur if such constraints were removed. Consistency of behaviour is more likely to occur if a cognitive reconceptualization of the traits as proposed by Mischel (1973; 1979 etc.) is taken into consideration. This contention has been challenged (Bem, 1983; Funder, 1983; Epstein, 1983) though not very convincingly.

2.3.3 Cognitive Considerations

Mischel (1973) had previously called for a cognitive reconceptualization of the underlying consistency of behaviour. His attempt was to provide an integration of the researches that has been going on in related areas like social learning etc. He wanted the trait concepts to be replaced with equally individualistic 'person variables' such as : (1) Cognitive and behavioural construction strategies, (2) Encoding strategies, (3) Behaviour-outcome and stimulus-outcome expectancies, (4) Subjective stimulus values, and (5) Self-regulatory systems and plans. He mentioned the progress made in the area in 1979. On their own merit, the concepts look quite reasonable and promising. However, an empirical problem that crops up is that research into those concepts is mostly possible using younger children. It has not been used extensively with adults to show whether those concepts can be used with them equally discriminatively.

2.3.4 Summing Up

When one tries to unravel the complexity of human behaviour, one must accept multitudes of alternatives. The sheer variations demonstrated by the number of theories of personality clearly highlight the contention. Not only it shows that various issues are involved, but also that there are multitudes of ways in which such issues can be conceptualized. Trait-theorists may sound like one united group of researchers but they are truly adherents of differing views of traits. Eysenck and Cattell being supporters of a genetic-deterministic view of trait-like consistency of behaviour, have researched extensively to link the so-called traits to biological bases. Hogan and others simply take traits to be shared or common descriptors. Then again there are various levels of extensity of trait names with no clearly defined hierarchical relationship. For example, extraversion is a more extensive trait term than sociability. Some are finicky about the choice of the term and object to the use of the term trait to concepts like 'friendliness' etc. as rather casual. The fact is, after Allport's (1937) marathon effort, trait theorists have not been able to provide a unified and integrated description of the trait concepts and their uses. Maddi (1981) has vehemently argued in favour of strong theorizing in the field of personality. It is time for the still stubborn hard-nosed empiricists to accept that without the theory and consensus among the researchers, the so-called empirical data cannot provide the answer to the vexing questions of understanding different concepts.

Attempts at integration have taken place at various levels. On one level, Kline's (1983) effort, through belated, is a step in the right direction. At least while fighting off the strong attacks from Bem and Mischel, trait theorists can seek solace in the findings that Cattell's Exvia turns out to be the identical twin of Eysenck's Extraversion. On another level Hampson *et al.*'s (1986) effort to constructing the trait hierarchy of breadth using trait as a concept has helped to clarify some issues. A recent research on MMPI showed a good agreement in the factor naming by a group of leading trait psychologists (Johnson *et al.*, 1984). But to the discerning there were enough disagreement to upset the apple cart.

Trait psychology is in need of a sweeping reorganization and integration not on an individual researcher's level but on a global basis. Without that trait theorists themselves must have realized that the information value of their studies even for other trait psychologists can be very low. Apart from that there is also a strong need to reconceptualize the trait so that the inconsistency problem is tackled in an elegant way.

2.4 Other Alternatives

Buss & Craik (1981; 1983) try to conceptualize personality through the Act-Frequency analyses. From this point of view, to judge a person as extraverted would mean counting the number of trait-like behaviours shown. They supported

Hampshire's (1953) contention which was : "When someone's dispositions is in dispute, the final and conclusive argument must lie on the balance of one set of actual incidents against another set of actual incidents" (p. 35). From their point of view, traits are merely summary descriptions of behaviour as it happened up to that time. There is no causality implied. And yet, from actuarial grounds, trait scores could be used for prediction of behaviour. Two of the important steps, therefore, were to classify the various traits indicative behaviour observed over a period of time and then to make a frequency analysis. In such a case, the demonstrated discrepancy in the consistency of behaviour would be a basically behavioural problem and not a dispositional one. It can easily be pointed out that the traditional inventory approach merely uses the act (reported, rather than demonstrated) frequency in its analysis. In fact, each item in a test can be broken down into various acts and a frequency calculation can be made if any specific behavioural predication is to be attempted. There are definite psychological and conceptual problems involved which stops us from observing actual behaviour as our fundamental data. Unlike the ethologists who pry open every intimate detail of animals' behaviour (no fear of invasion of privacy there!), trait psychologists have to fall back on the ubiquitous pen and paper reporting of the behaviour. The jugglery of the statistical analysis will then play its role, not necessarily enhancing our understanding of the issues at stake.

Another approach suggested by Lamiell (1981) is the idiothetic approach. He pointed out the difference between the approaches of differential psychology, and personality psychology. The former is the approach developed along the line of ability testing where an individual's performance is compared to a reference group's performance. The latter framework, as Lamiell states, "is grounded in the basic notion that an individual's personality is best described in terms of information about what the person tends to do — not in direct contrast with what others tend to do, but in contrast with what that person tend not to do but could do" (p. 281). Further elaborating on the processes involved he stated, "The point is that the comparability of persons along common attributes is not critical to the systematic. empirical characterization of any one person's action at a given point of time. The essence of idiothetic measurement is not that it rejects the assumption of universal applicability (cf. Bem & Allen 1974; Kenrick & Stringfield 1980) but it renders this assumption immaterial" (p. 283).

The term idiothetic needs to be appreciated as an essential bridge, not merely a compromise, between the nomothetic approach and the idiographic approach. It is an attempt to study the individual as an individual with idiosyncratic consistencies that may or may not tally with the psychometrician's conceptualization of the world. Nunnally (1967) stated, "The idiographists may be entirely correct, but if they are, it is a sad day for psychology. Idiography is an anti-science point of view: it discourages the search for general laws and instead encourages the description of particular phenomena (people)" (p. 472). Need it be pointed out that such a view-point, which unfortunately dominated psychometrics, not only lacks an understanding of psychology, but of philosophy and science as well. Supporters of nomothetic approach study only a small fraction of humanity for some common attributes and generalize to the whole universe. It is a far greater inferential leap though admittedly more implied than explicitly stated. With the same inferential principle one can study an individual's individuality and discover how much of it he shares with others. There is a strong logic behind the conception of general human law and its particular use with an individual with varying degrees of error. At the same time, there is absolutely nothing anti-scientific about inferring from an observed individual phenomenon and then generalizing to a group as proposed by Lamiell. The PI approach is very much sympathetic to Lamiell's proposition that aims at integration rather than at unnecessary division. The approach, however, appreciates the use of some theory based constructs in the traditional method and aims to capitalize on the various viewpoints as elaborated elsewhere. It needs to be pointed out that Lamiell, in a small study, showed how individuals could have varying degrees of consistencies on four dimensions obtained through multi-dimensional scaling of behavioural descriptions.

Bem & Funder (1978) used the adapted Q-sort techniques to study the idiosyncratic processes involved in self-description and the conceptualization of the environment in which various behaviours take place. Green (1980) has showed that it boils down to a simple additive model as proposed by the inventories. The use of an individual's inconsistency as a moderator variable to predict behaviour as proposed by Bem & Allen (1974) has been criticized by Tellegen *et. al.* (1982) on methodological grounds. The inconsistencies that the PI approach aims to tap would, therefore, be handled in a different way as described in detail later.

Such approaches give importance to both situation and trait in determining individual behaviour. It must be emphasized that the situation they are talking about is not the situation described objectively by its salient features but as inferred/perceived by each individual as distinct from others. This is the situational study the PI approach strongly promotes. Confusion on this has led to an apparent opposition between social and trait psychologists. For example, Kline lamented, "egalitarian Zeitgeist of giving importance to situation has a strong hold over British Psychological establishment, and research funds for trait studies of personality are not easily come-by, which, in part, account for the dearth of experimental evidence". The lament obliquely highlights the importance of two things: (1) Funds in devising tests and (2) The apparent opposition of traits and situation. On the first count, the PI approach scores heavily against situational tests and the so-called objective observations. There is always the mundane "dollar criteria" (Brogden & Taylor, 1950), the cost-pay off matrix, to bring the high-flying research idealists to down-to-earth reality. Paper and pencil tests such as the inventories have been the cheapest method of acquiring information to date. The second ground has been the source of discontent even among trait psychologists. Barring the followers of Eysenck and Cattell (which logically should include them as well) there are not many psychologists who are simply willing to hand over their rights of deciding the kind of persons they are to genetics on a platter. They are not willing to do that to the situations either. There is more to an adult's personality than a mere sum of passive reactions to the environment or the gradual unfolding of biological endowments. There is an acute lack of an integrative theory of traits which could combine the various studies and bring contending view points together in building a stronger trait theory. It is attempted here through a reconceptualization of the trait versus situation problem.

The Integrative View Point

2.5 Preliminary Analysis of some Contentions

It is undeniable that individual differences exist at the time of birth or even before it. These differences can be quite discernible even in fraternal twins. Some hypothesize that such differences are due to the genes that yield some particular type of nervous system. Eysenck has stimulated a large number of researches in this area. By sheer weight of number of research papers and books published, Eysenck's contention can be deemed almost inviolable. His research has been cumulative, anchored on solid physiology, and has provided a few hallmarks which can guide one's thinking as well as research. His super factors namely, Extraversion, Neuroticism and Psychoticism (PEN) are deemed to be the essence of human personality. As Kline & Barrett's (1983) study showed, the super factors seem to crop up more often than any other factors in the analysis. This must be deemed amazing when the problems of factor analysis like marker variables, methods of rotation and extraction, the psychological indeterminacy of Thurstonian simple structure, and factor naming etc. are taken into consideration. But on the other hand, it can be seen that such results necessarily follow from the ubiquity of the concepts as explained below.

Extraversion mostly refers to outgoing activities centering round the peripheral nervous system, the conation. Neuroticism, which is used interchangeably with emotionality shows the affective tone via the autonomic nervous system. It can be seen that the old trichotomy of human experience into cognition, affection, and conation had been very useful in the way Extraversion and Neuroticism were defined. In contrast, Psychoticism banks heavily on unconventionality, a predominantly psychological concept with strong social overtones. Incidentally, these are the aspects that would stand out in day to day living conditions. One may have the acquaintance of a person for a long time without being any wiser about his altruism and honesty etc. But as regards his out-going behaviour, worrying and unconventionality, one is more likely to come up with some behavioural evidence. This logic is true even in the writing of the items in which such underlying implications could be discerned. As factors are deemed to be the link among an assorted group of items correlating with each other, the process of factor naming is quite likely to capitalize on such discernible aspects.

These arguments are not against the view point of Eysenck as far as the basic structure of personality is concerned. These are to clarify that, independent of the so-called solid evidence of biology, there are strong psychological bases for the acceptance of the system and that also makes the EPQ a very useful instrument to start with. We lose more by contending about the ultimate power of genetics, society, and the self given the level of sophistication involved in psychological measuring instruments. It would be much better if the integrative view as described below is considered.

2.5.1 The Theory of Opposing Forces

Allport (1937) was impressed by the fact that there are 18,000 trait descriptive words in English vocabulary. He inferred the great importance given to the individual for his actions. Edwards (1957) was impressed with the fact that such a large number of different trait terms could be seen to be varying on a single dimension of social desirability. Had he been a bit inclined towards social psychology he would have inferred the sheer force of society in determining individual's action. And it does not require much thinking to be impressed by the fact that each of those trait terms has a twin having similarity of behavioural connotations but opposing social desirability. One needs just to open his eyes and take a relatively detached view of religion, politics, civics; ethics etc. to see that in each and every sphere of human life, there is no consensus regarding any particular action being unambiguous and absolutely correct. There are always two aspects supported and highlighted by opposing parties scrupulously refraining from the other aspect. That has resulted in different observations, *e.g.*, "When you do it, it is tactfulness but when others do it, it becomes sheer cowardice. When you help someone, you are being kind, but when others do it they are simply showing off." When taken away from the social milieu in which any behaviour takes place and abstracted, a trait may seem completely desirable, such as honesty and helpfulness, etc. But in the social life from which all trait inferences are made, such purified social desirability which everybody accept in its extremeness is non-existent. Being absolutely honest is hardly desirable for the majority of the cases. Lot of what we call 'sophistication' can be re-labeled as lying and a lot of uncouth behaviour can be seen to be simply honest and straight forward. An extremely honest person will invariably harm a genuinely repentant or situationally overwhelmed person. Shakespeare has immortalized the conflict in his play, "The Merchant of Venice". When Shylock insisted on having his pound of flesh on a justified and legal basis, Portia had to resort to the juxtaposition of mercy and justice showing two desirable qualities at loggerheads. Though the case was not won on that ground it must have been a real tough decision for the learned judges. The push and pull of opposing forces take place inevitably in every aspect of human interaction. Our legal system, thankfully, are adaptable to such contingencies though, regrettably, our trait concepts are not.

Even in less charged situation than the one described, a complex interaction among the opposing forces takes place. Often the opposing forces are not just two but could be many more. An individual may highlight one dimension through ignorance or deliberate underplaying of the other dimension and act accordingly. But any extreme deviation on the part of one individual makes the other dimension conspicuous by its absence. When a person becomes highly extraverted, he would impinge on the privacy of others, thereby, highlighting the show-off or nosiness of the trait in the eyes of the other individuals. This would start the social pressure to rectify the deviation in the opposing dimension. It is complex, in the sense people tend to highlight the dimension according to whether they describe a friend, an enemy, or themselves, etc. The extraversion dimension becomes 'warm' with friends but becomes 'show off' with an opponent. There is no law of logic that could decide the correctness of any of the descriptions. We need to realize that there are more realities than one and therefore, there is no true score as conceptualized in psychometrics. We need to keep our eyes open for different realities and to look beyond statistically usable concepts.

2.5.2 Socialization and the Growth of Traits

The juxtaposition described above does not occur in the realm of taking decision in the adulthood. From a very early stage of growth the child comes across such contradictions as a part of growing pains of being civilized; falling in line. In order to grow up into the social system, one has to balance the opposing forces in every dimension of social interaction. Therefore, an analysis of the process of socialization will help in better appreciation of the integrative view point. There is no denying the fact that even in new born or yet-to-be-born babies there exist individual differences in reactivity, appearance and needs, etc. that can be accepted as genetically determined. But that rudimentary personality is no way comparable to the complexity of an adult's extraversion. It is all so rigorously scientific to demonstrate that the extraverts have high reaction time and figural after-effects, etc. But when it comes to real life, nobody cares to know about an individual's figural after-effects. It is what he does in the company of fellow human beings that determines his extraversion. But, as will be shown later, such inherent differences might go a long way in sustaining the differences till adulthood, not because the social reinforcements are ineffective but because they were never used in the first place.

Soon after the baby is born, the socialization process starts. A happy, smiling baby begets more attention than an unhappy cry baby. This reinforces a kind of stranger anxiety that is most likely to lead to introversion. As soon as the baby is capable of taking instructions, the do's and don'ts creep into his/her life. Any patient mother or father who has tried to teach the children the rules of behaviour must have appreciated the absurdity and embarrassment of stretching any rule to its extreme. The thin dividing line between the do and the don't do is not apparent to the child. Thus, the child learns, in the hard way, that he should be friendly but not too much, independent but not too much, quiet but not too quiet and so on. So whatever may be the genetic endowments, the child learns to toe the line as a matter of learning the tricks of survival because he cannot possibly create his own situations. The society supports and reinforces moderation because in many ways that provides the least resultant disequilibrium from all the dimensions. But the social reinforcements are not administered as pellets of food in animal laboratory. The more chance a child has of getting away, psychologically and physically, from the reinforcing or punishing situation, the less he will be amenable to the reinforcement contingencies. In addition, the less the busy mothers and/or significant others have time to spend with the child and provide reinforcement, the less the child will be amenable to such forces.

2.5.3 The Processes of Social Reinforcement

Nobody really sits with the child ready to administer reinforcement or punishment as soon as a behaviour is shown as in shaping experiments. Most of the time society allows a range of behaviour indicative of any trait within which the children are permitted to vary. Children whose behaviour falls within that range are accepted as being "OK" and are left alone. It is only when the child becomes extremely introverted or extraverted (for example) that the adults get worried and bring in reinforcements into the picture to remedy the deviation. Of course, in different cultures and individual families different degrees of deviation are tolerated. An adolescent in India who does not show interest in the opposite sex would be accepted as normal. Such behaviour, if shown by their adolescent off-spring, would have many British parents very worried.

It is worth noting the informal reinforcement that takes place in the day-to-day life that suppresses or facilitates the demonstration of trait-like behaviour. A child, being active, can take the first step towards greeting somebody and is in turn greeted by others. In subsequent encounters, such previous behaviour creates an expectancy in both the parties which makes the behaviour more likely to occur. The child would also be encouraged to try similar behaviour in similar conditions with different persons thus providing the frequency of occurrence essential to the formation of a habit. In contrast, an introvert can find difficulty in taking the first step in greeting someone and, therefore, decreasing the probability of such a behaviour occurring later. Expectancy plays a very big role in shaping one's behaviour. This is how the social reinforcement intermingles with genetic disposition and produces the habitual mode of responding that is subsequently identified as a trait. This conception does not imply any inevitability of such traits. Any adult can easily change his characteristic mode of responding if he decides to change. The self-concept of individual most often plays the paramount role. But it is not very often that one is required to change his habits that drastically. Thus, we find the behaviour of the persons repeated with apparent consistency. More importantly, adults have the chance of choosing the company they keep thereby overriding the need to change their trait. The person of power in our societies can afford the luxury of publicized idiosyncrasies that transcends the situations like the Churchillean pipe. Lesser mortals like university sophomores or research students are more likely to vary as per their perception of the varying situation. For them, it would be a matter of survival or at least a gateway to better life. Therefore, a majority would fall in line rather than try to establish their individuality.

2.5.4 Applying Theory to Oneself

Every social situation has components of desirability as well as many other dimensions. Individuals respond to the situation as per their own perception of it. Sometime this may tally with the salient feature of the situation that the psychometricians try to use for comparability in normative research. But it is quite likely to be different in different individuals' cases. Thus, a high degree of error of inference is very much expected in the normative research. A personal example would clarify the matters. Prof. Kline, who happens to be the author's supervisor, is avowedly a rank-order-position-maintaining introvert. Not only that he regularly discovers the factor of extraversion in data but also he sees a lot of consistency in characterizing persons as extraverted. The author, in spite of a thorough study of extraversion and self-analysis could not find for himself a stable place in that trait. While in the company of his friends, the author likes to participate actively in the proceedings. And yet, as required in an academic life, he finds no discomfiture in spending hours together sans friendship and sans extraversion in the company of books and own thoughts. From a purely biological point of view it is difficult to explain such wild fluctuation without resorting to the theory of a wildly fluctuating yet stable nervous system. Such a conception is not required when one uses the integrative view point.

There is a strong possibility that Prof. Kline's self-concept as an introvert lends strong support to his other aspects. He is certainly not the most ferocious sight when, being in an expansive mood, he flexes his muscles. Struggling to be five feet tall in his shoes, if it can thus be stated, he does not have much to support extraversion physically. Psychologically and intellectually, he would find less use of extraversion. Introversion adds to his image as a research oriented professor (as observed by some of the author's friends). In contrast, the author is built like a street fighter (the appearance somewhat marred by the thick glasses he has to wear). Physically the author likes to let go in sports and other pastimes. Psychologically also, his limited ability but strong inclination towards histrionics has found a useful ally in extraversion. Before this neo-Sheldonian analogy is taken too far, it must be mentioned that when the author works, he even finds such pleasantries as greetings and bidding good-byes a positive nuisance and refrains from it. A love for reading also ensures that some amount of privacy and free time is actively sought. This makes such fluctuation on the trait of extraversion on the part of the author, hopefully, understandable. Strait-jacketing of such fluctuations into a rigid trait concept would have caused unnecessary hardships.

The above analysis was not made to prove or disprove the existence of extraversion as a trait. It is made as an acceptance of the fact that in individual cases we do find variation on a trait dimension. Consistency is, therefore, not an obvious phenomenon but an abstracted trend amidst variation that is achieved with varying degrees of success. There have been too many evidences of fluctuation of persons across situation, to tackle them on methodological grounds. From the psychometrician's point of view, a better approach will be to locate and measure the variation for further use than to stick obstinately to the idea of fixed traits as elaborated below.

2.5.5 About the Fixity of Traits

As a continuation of the idea of opposing dimensions in every trait indicative behaviour which forces the individual throughout his growth period, it is theorized that an adult's position on a trait dimension is a dynamic equilibrium between opposing forces of social desirability. Each is a personal and unique resultant of the resolution of double approach-avoidance conflicts, taking his growing self-concept and biological endowments into consideration. At this point also it must be pointed out that the double approach-avoidance conflicts are rather simplified version of the reality where more than two alternatives often co-exist.

Under a dynamic conception of trait it will be wrong to expect that a person who has a high total score will show a greater amount of trait indicative behaviour in every situation than someone who has a low score. The individual will show normally distributed pattern of trait indicative behaviour around their average behaviour. The average score can only be meaningful if the variation of the intra-individual distribution of trait-like behaviour is small. When inter-individual variations are considered there should be a lot of overlap between two scores. If two persons, one scoring high and the other scoring low on the extraversion scale, find themselves in similar situations then they will show a range of behaviour that can be seen to be overlapping. The relative position on any situation will depend on the individual's idiosyncratic conception of the situation. Such conceptions can hardly be theorized to be invariant across situations given the number of factors that govern human behaviour at any particular time. If the individual's individuality is to be respected, then it can be seen that at some point a low scoring person can actually show more or higher trait indicative behaviour than one who apparently scored higher in the total. It is not necessary to imply that such relationship to be cross-situationally pervasive in order to be able to show that people, in general, do not maintain their rank order positions on any trait dimension. It also does not negate the possibility of a group of persons, having low variability, maintaining their rank order. The suggestion is merely that there are many more persons who vary or change widely on any dimension than are the persons who remain in a relatively constant position on any trait. Even if the two groups are equally numbered, the presence of varying persons will make the discovery of relatively constant person that much difficult simply because we will not be looking for them as and when we come across some of them.

A trait is merely a strong habit built through the intricate relationships among the genetic endowment, social reinforcement and the growing self-concept. (Big deal, every psychologist knows it! But, hang on, because they don't know what to do about it!) A trait is consistent to the extent any learnt habit is consistent, being more or less permanent with varying degrees of resistance to extinction. A trait is inconsistent to the extent it is learnt and therefore can be unlearnt. A high variability on one dimension may ultimately imply that the respondent did not find similarity among the situations as was visualized by the test-developer. From another angle it may mean that a particular trait may not form a salient feature of the individual's self-concept. In such cases, it will be worthwhile to look for consistency at a different level of the trait or a different trait altogether. For example, an attempt to explain the author's inconsistency in the trait of extraversion can be made by thinking of an "extremism" trait that transcends the need to be either introvert or extravert as required by the psychometricians. (In any case, just who in psychology are they to tell me what I am supposed to be ?). However, this trait would not again be cross-situationally consistent. If it fits into the self-concept of a person being adaptable, it would in fact encourage inconsistencies (flexibility, dynamism, more human!). So it will be better to measure the variation and leave the judgement of consistency to the person looking for the application of trait scores.

2.5.6 On Consistency

Lest any desirability be associated with the concept of consistency, it needs to be clarified that consistency can also mean rigidity depending on what perspective one takes. In fact, persons showing greater variation on a trait could be well suited to a job. In the ability context, Spearman, in a rare flash of humour, stated that a high fluctuation is very good in air plane designer but can be disastrous in an airplane pilot. It can also be possible in the personality contest. To be a psychotherapist, being ambivert and less fluctuating will be good criteria but for success as a salesman, a high fluctuation with moderately high extraversion will be more useful to adopt to the needs of the different clientele. A variation score would, therefore, become a useful parameter of personality rather than a nuisance (error) as has been thought of so far. Such information will extend the information revealed by a single trait score.

There can be an alternative explanation of the demonstrated inconsistencies in behaviour as noted elsewhere. Hampson *et. al.* (1986), in their study, pointed out that the apparent confusion from the lack of consistency of behaviour as indicative of a trait accrue from the fact that trait descriptive terms have differing breadth. Extraversion as a trait descriptive term covers a broad band and, therefore, would be expected to yield a low consistency of behaviour across situation. Logically such concepts as trait breadth should relate to the inconsistency (error) to be anticipated in the observed behaviour via the steps of abstraction needed for its conceptualization.

While there is some strength in the argument, it cannot be denied that an individual has his/her own idiosyncratic reasons for which he shows fluctuations of behaviour. That is the sign of his individuality, his trademark, the very essence of his being. Everybody likes to be liked for his individuality. Somehow, this aspect seems to be completely missed by the psychometricians. In this context, instead of asking the questions "Whether consistent or inconsistent?" a better strategy will be to ask "How consistent is consistent?" or rather "How inconsistent is consistent?" There are always some fluctuations being demonstrated by all the individuals even in the narrowest of trait descriptive terms. We deliberately ignore some fluctuations and see the essential consistencies. In fact, we know that people have various degrees of tolerance towards inconsistency in different traits. A single instance of dishonesty can ruin many instances of honest behaviour while, in the case of persons we love, we could tolerate more flippant behaviour. People do set different standards for different persons such as their leaders, their friends, keeper of the corner shop, and the milkman, etc. Instead of characterizing someone as consistent or inconsistent from a personal (psychometrician's) point of view, if an index of consistency can be provided for the trait under consideration, the person concerned could then decide how much inconsistency either he can tolerate or is positively looking for and take decision, accordingly.

The question one can raise at this point is if most of the people vary so much, how come tests measuring the traits show high test-retest reliability, as does the EPQ, for example? It is very unlikely that the tests sample only those persons who do not fluctuate. The answer lies in the way in which the inventories are developed. When the idea of personality consist of a combination of rock steady traits, any variation is frowned upon as measurement error (test unreliability). The traditional methods of using factor analysis of the items, or item-total correlation etc. ensure that test items having low correlation (high variation) are unceremoniously weeded out. Items powerful enough to elicit more or less the same kind of responses across different administrations are retained. The other possibility is that the testing situation itself is highly charged with demand characteristics (Orne, 1962) which tends to elicit the expected behaviour, repeatedly. It is no wonder that we do find high test-retest correlation (at least in some high-profile psychological tests). But the fact that in spite of all these regimentation and rigorous use of statistics to wipe out test unreliability, tests are still reported to be having on an average of .5 test-retest reliability shows that we were looking at wrong factors to explain test unreliability. We have not gained much in conceptualizing traits as fixed and, thereby, having to explain a large fluctuation of scores as a limitation of the test. An alternative approach of sampling some fluctuation and then taking a decision about the limit (a sort of Difference Limen as studied in the psychophysical methods) inside which it will be deemed that the person is consistent may turn out to be more useful. This is precisely what is attempted through the PI approach.

2.6. *The Contributions of the PI Approach*

Another important aspect of the attempt to find the consistency of traits is the keeping of reference points similar if not identical so that the comparison used in nomothetic studies can be meaningful. As discussed earlier, users of personality inventories feel that they have adequately taken care of the subjectivity that creeps into projective tests. Such faith is misplaced as the assumption is psychologically not true. Individuals will have their own meaning attached to the various concepts no matter what the actual trait items or the instructions are. A theoretical analysis of a few items of the EPQ will illustrate the point. For example, the question like "Do you believe in the institution of marriage?" will not be perceived similarly by a person who had the experience of a particularly bad marriage as the person who had better experience of marriage. His negative response to the question will not therefore indicate Psychoticism or aggressiveness but simply his own condition. Moreover, in the western countries where the divorce rate is very high, such a response would rather be taken as a statement of fact rather than Psychoticism, aggressiveness or even unconventionality. In contrast, another person who gives priority to real love as the basis of marriage over institutionalization respond similarly (saying 'No') but for the opposite reasons. Similarly, answering the question "Do you love going to the parties?" would entail remembering the experience of different parties with different connotations. So, far from every one referring to an abstracted but comparable concept of parties (dictionary definition?) each will be referring to different situations. Accepting the fact that diversity is the essence of human experience and behaviour, its understanding and comparison is made easier if the phenomenon one refers to is, at least objectively, the same. This is aimed to be achieved through the PI approach.

As mentioned earlier, the construction of tests under the PI approach entails descriptions of various situations for reference. They are deemed to be analogous of actual situations providing a cheap alternative to the situational tests. There should normally be five to eight such stories to which the respondents refer when taking the test. Each of the stories is followed by items regarding the stories. The items can be scored within a limited range of values. The total of such score will show where the individual stands *vis-à-vis* the other respondents. In addition, the fluctuation of scores across the stories (situations) in this approach will not be the ubiquitous error but an integral part of the dynamic process of individual's construal of and adaptation to different social situations.

2. 6. 1. The Computation of Dynamism Indices

The expectation regarding the development of the test (named PIAPEN) was that from among the stories about 4-5 stories would be selected. Each of the stories could provide the possibility of a sizeable score (5-7) for at least one of the traits. It did not require all the tests to be capable of measuring all the traits with equal efficiency. In any case the test could then be conceived as a combination of 4-5 tests each consisting of a story and about 5-7 relevant trait indicative items for each of the three personality factors. That would provide a range of possible scores for each of the respondent over and above the total score that would be the sum of the components. These components are not just an arbitrary cutting down of a total score. On the contrary, the components provide the context of the total without which the trait concept has already been shown to be facing difficulty in retaining its scientific viability. This description makes it clear that each of the stories that are retained after the item analysis would yield scores varying from 0 to the highest possible (5-7) for at least one of the traits when administered on a sample of subjects. From this data, various Dynamism Indices (DIs) can be computed depending on the interest of the researcher. None of the indices implies any superiority over the others nor are they deemed to be exhaustive of the possibilities of different meaningful computations. It is not merely like playing around with numbers as one does while using the various method of factor analysis. Each of those has important connotations and derived from the same response highlight the truism, described earlier at length, that there are many ways of conceptualizing the same behaviour.

One type of DI can be computed by analyzing how far a person varies from his personal average when his performance on the relevant stories is taken into consideration. That would be the idiographic DI of the person on a particular trait. The problem which would arise from the lack of equal range in the tests (which is only to be expected from a fixed item selection criteria for all the stories) can be tackled by scaling so that comparing scores over the situation can be meaningful. Another possible use is the computation of the ratio between what was possible in a test and what was actually scored by an individual. This ratio could be used as an idiothetic DI as proposed by Lamiell.

The third possibility is the one of calculating an individual's deviation score that will be somewhat analogous to the calculation of deviation IQ scores. In each story the standard score of a person's performance *vis-à-vis* the normative group can be computed. Calculating the average deviation of the person across all stories will provide a good index of how far the person deviates in relation to a reference group. This will provide a base to decide on a person's variation, not on its own but in relation to the base rate fluctuation one would expect in a reference group. The test-user can decide on his cut-off point. This DI will be most useful for normative research.

A fourth kind of DI can be computed by scaling the different dimensions of the stories themselves. From that, given the highest scores possible for each trait, a score as reflective of the personality of the situation (in the style of ecological psychology) can be estimated. From that the total deviation of a person would reflect how far the person is varying according to demand characteristics of the situation. Social and ecological psychologists are likely to find this particular index useful. This index is, therefore, distinctly different from the individual's idiosyncratic variation which was mentioned above and emphasized in the dynamic conception of the trait.

One can, with ingenuity and story writing ability provide further improvisations and adapt the tests for specialized uses. In any case, the PI approach, as it stands, can provide four important DIs to conduct further research and base decisions on. The only and all important necessity is that, after the item selection, a reasonable number of items should be left to provide the score variation in at least a majority of the stories. Of course, if such an attempt fails one can attempt further by using multiple keying or the five point Likert-type rating scale format, etc. In any case, the PI approach holds a lot of promises. It is left for the empirical studies to prove how much of that can be realized.

2.7. *The Kernel of Truth*

The traditional concept of rigid traits was yielding too much of test error and the attendant human frustration which sadly has been identified as a necessary and inevitable nuisance in the sphere of measurement of traits. It need not necessarily be so. The PI approach, with necessary and perfectly logical formulation of a flexible trait concept reconceptualizes the error as an index of a person's dynamic adaptation as integral part of a more or less stable personality pattern. After years of stagnation, having reached the limits of the traditional concept of trait which seem to be having difficulty in providing adequate defence to a non-tenable position, it is high time a reconceptualized trait position is given the chance for furthering research through the PI approach.

The PI approach permits the computation of four (till now) Dynamism Indices as reflective of essential human dynamic adaptations. There have been various unrelated attempts to measure any one of them. Nowhere it was deemed possible that the differing points of view could utilize the same test for their own purposes without ascribing any ascendancy to their approach. It is strongly felt that a proper understanding of personality can be possible only if an integrative view of the different perspectives is taken and seen to be contributing more or less equally. The decision of using any one or more of those indices that must depend on the research need, personal problems etc. is left to the decision of the end-user.

"Did you ever make real life into a dream?", said the Earl, "Now just try. I've often amused myself that way."

Three

The Social Desirability Effect

3. The Initial Idea

It is difficult to find someone in psychometrics who, at least to some extent, does not know how undesirable the discovery of Social Desirability (hereinafter to be addressed as SD) effect has been to the attempt of psychometricians to discover the truth behind human personality using the inventory approach. Nobody questions the SD effect barring some incorrigible social psychologists. Once discovered, the test developer must do everything to counter the malady (the terminal bout of SDE) that afflicts the test lest it leads to ostracization from the scientific community. But given the state of the proposed anti-dotes, the only thing that a test developer can do about it is to start on a new test again, unless of course, it is a MMPI, a CPI or an EPQ, for example. In the animal farm of psychological tests, some tests are more equal than others. Tests having the pedigree can afford to look down upon the SD effect even when they affected by it and people will not notice it. Since a new test being developed under the PI approach cannot have such pedigree, the analysis of the virulence and pervasiveness of the SD effect is undertaken so that the final decision can left to the end-user.

To a great extent the initial conceptualization of the PI approach owed its origin to this effect. It was deemed that the PI approach, having the subtlety of items and the projective nature of the stories, would be the ultimate answer to the problem of tackling the SD effect. This study was initially aimed at developing a test as equivalent of one established inventory and to show the efficacy of such a test in being proof against the SDE while the original test shows the lack of such resistance. But a critical look at the social desirability effect revealed many ad hoc suppositions bereft of any clear reasons or evidence. Some of the prominent advices have been analyzed which shows the comical situation hardly befitting an area of scientific research. The role of social desirability is reconceptualized in line with the dynamic conceptualization of trait.

3.1. The Discovery

Edwards (1957) rediscovered an interesting phenomenon. He called it the Social Desirability Effect (SDE). In the Introductory chapter of his book which publicized the SDE, after a brief analysis of the diversities involved in trait description and the statements used to tap it, Edwards contended, "Consider now the population of statements that might be used in describing personality. It is my contention that each of these statements can be characterized in terms of its position on a single dimension. I call this dimension social desirability-undesirability dimension or more briefly, the social desirability dimension. I believe, for example, that it is possible to obtain a scale value for any personality statement such that the scale value indicates the position of the statement on the social desirability continuum, relative, of course, to other statements. It should be emphasized that I am not saying that these same statements may not fall along various other dimensions. I am contending that regardless of the multidimensional nature of personality statements, with respect to content, it is still possible to describe each one in terms of its position on the social desirability continuum. The social desirability continuum appears to me to be the most important single dimension on which to locate personality statements. The imnortance of the dimension rests in the fact that, if we know the position of a statement on it, we can then predict, with a high degree of accuracy, the proportion of individuals who will say, in self-description, that the statement does describe them" (p.3).

The pervasiveness of the SD dimension thus established, Edwards described the procedure as follows : "The social desirability scale value of a personality statement has been defined as a value that is obtained as a result of performing certain operations upon a set of observations made under specific conditions. The observations are the judgements of social desirability made by the subjects in the group. The operations are those of a particular psychological scaling method. The specified conditions are the instructions given to the members of the judging group"(p.7).

Then Edwards did some soul-searching (as any psychologist involved in the discovery of universality in human behaviour should do) regarding the representativeness of the judges, the items and even the scaling method (!). Those who feel that societies vary both at micro and macro level and that, therefore, the related desirabilities would be expected to vary widely would, no doubt, sympathize with him. But the judges, or rather the hard experimental data came up with a thumping vindication of the Edwardian effort in search of the universal (precious few of its kind in psychology). One hundred and fifty two judges rated 140 items from the Edwards Personal Preference Schedule (EPPS) on a 9 point scale of social desirability varying from 1 (extremely undesirable) to 9 (extremely desirable). In an impressive display of unanimity the judges agreed across age and sex (two most often-used but least understood variables) (Edwards 1953a). Of course, there were irritating items with large deviations (less agreement). But as the item analysis so efficiently does it, the items were weeded out before the scale was formed. This would otherwise look like a piece of research demonstrating how society brings conformity, to some extent, in the reported perception of values. But that inference would not have been as sensational as the one that was to follow later.

The second stage in the identification of the SD syndrome came in the chapter entitled "Probability of Endorsement and Social Desirability Scale Value". Various studies were reported to show impressive correlation between the social desirability scale values (SDSVs) of the items and the probability that those will be endorsed, endorsement referring to the fact of saying yes to desirable dimension and no to undesirable dimension. The identity of this relationship is to be inferred from the very initial conceptualization of social desirability as varying continuously from highly desirable to highly undesirable.

Edwards, however, was magnanimous in giving the honour of initial discovery of the syndrome to Meehl & Hathway (1946). The latter were upset about the susceptibility of personality inventories to "faking" which was supposed to be a conscious distortion of scores. Lest somebody pulls them up for defamation, they also showed concern for unconscious self-deception and role-playing. They lamented that this occurs with subjects who seemed (how?) to be quite "honest" and "sincere" in their response. Between the two aspects of faking Edwards found unconscious faking more useful: safe for him but potent for the psychometricians. He stated, "Faking good on personality inventories, without special instruction to do so, I would consider equivalent to the tendency to give socially desirable responses in self-description. It is this tendency, of course, that the SD was designed to measure" (p. 57). Having such specifications, the SD becomes almost impossible to tackle, and has since served as the free-floating anxiety of the inventory world. But such a role for the SD effect was not consistent with the conclusion.

Edwards concluded, "As I have pointed out elsewhere (1953a), it is possible that the trait or items which are judged socially desirable are those that are fairly common or dominant among the members of a group. If a characteristic is prevalent or dominant in a group, it will perhaps be judged desirable. If this is the case, we might expect statements relating to desirable traits to be endorsed more frequently than those relating to undesirable ones.

It is also possible that the trait indicated by the statement with a high social desirability scale value is not prevalent or dominant in a group, but that subjects are responding to the statement trying, consciously or unconsciously to give a good impression. He may therefore respond to the statements in such a way to attribute to himself more of the socially desirable traits and fewer of the socially undesirable traits than he would if his personality were evaluated in terms of some other criteria. This would also account for the relationship found between probability of endorsement and social desirability scale value" (p.86).

The conclusion is restrained and can be seen to be perfectly logical and balanced, perhaps even unfairly so. Unfairly, because, without any intellectual ascendancy implied for the stand point, we tend to judge everything as good and true etc. unless proved otherwise. There is no reason why it should change when the evidence is not logically convincing however impressive the agreement among the raters be. In other words, it needs to be proved that people are faking when they give SD response in a test. Unfortunately, this aspect has been ignored and somewhere somehow the faking explanation gained ascendancy over the former explanation. From that day onwards, this phenomenon as well as some theoretically and logically related concepts like need for approval (Crowne & Marlowe, 1964), self-disclosure (Jourard, 1979)and dissimulation etc. has been extensively studied in the attempt to plug this loophole which has rendered the inventory method almost useless.

Somehow the SD microbe seemed resistant to all preventive manipulations proving the futility of the exercises. The assumption behind these attempts was that if a probability-of-occurrence scale of behaviour under consideration is to be developed then it would show a high negative correlation with SD responding. Walsh *et. al.* (1969) showed that barring the methodological limitation involved in such an estimate, the judged occurrence of socially desirable behaviour correlates highly with the probability of endorsement. As they concluded, "Behaviour which occurs frequently tends to be socially desirable and frequently endorsed and *vice versa.* People not only do not endorse personality items representing socially undesirable behaviour, they also do not, in the eyes (or view) of their peers, perform the behaviours" (p.622). This study has obviously not allayed the fear of the troubled minds. The virulence image has left its indelible mark.

3.2. SD in Projective Tests

Edwards, as a continuation, exposed the limitation of the then best known inventories. He, however, left projective techniques alone. In fact, his prescription for remedy itself ran on inventory lines. By default, it would seem that the projective tests were somehow found not susceptible to the SD effect. The sheer absence of studies showing such relationship testifies in favour of such a contention. But there is no *a priori* ground for this gap when SD is seen in proper perspective. Pictures can be as socially desirable as the statements about one can be. In the name of research, one can show the children the picture of a small boy in a sexually intimate posture with an elderly woman, possibly with a elderly person's head lying somewhere in the vicinity (to discover the presence of Oedipus complex). It is not being done because it will be socially undesirable. In test development terms, it implies that people will not come up with vivid imagination, showing their traits in full colour to the discerning eyes of the test users if it evokes socially undesirable response even when used as a narrative and not self description.

There is as much of SD effect in projective tests as there is in any other forms of data collection including the inventories. Of course, from Edwards's point of view, a social desirability scale for the projective pictures would not have yielded the impressive agreement of the judges because the implications of those responses would be far from clear. But this is so merely because the pictures in the projective tests are analogous to the inventory items falling in the so-called neutral range of the SD scale. One cannot fake good because the alternatives are many and being good in those cases is not singularly defined. But one can easily "fake not-so-bad" by referring to human love, sympathy, and altruism while scrupulously avoiding sex and violence. If the items or, rather more correctly, the responses they yield are subjected to SDSV analysis, we are quite likely to come up with the startling discovery that the responses deemed more or less to be desirable are the responses that many respondents actually give. In fact, the misleading contention regarding the resistance of projective tests can be dangerous when wrongly used. In a clinical set up, rapport is invariably established. There is less need for defence mechanism and the role of SD is underplayed. But any faith in some sort of inherent resistance to SD, just because the test happens to be projective, will lead to misleading conclusions. A person having access to books on projective techniques and having a general idea about scoring will have unfair advantage over others in the conventional sense. This contention is based on the case of a serial-killer who faked multiple personality. As he had studied psychological testing he could do the faking with telling effect. He was, unfortunately, supported by a psychiatrist who mistakenly believed that a projective test cannot be faked. It took the brilliance of Orne to discover the drama behind this case and expose the serial-killer. Not all of us are blessed with that kind of social intelligence. But, all of us have enough intelligence to know the fact: The projective tests can also be faked.

3.3 The Fight for Survival

So, where do all those expositions leave us? There is no remedy; only some preventive measures being available with various doses of optimism. Some psychometricians aim to tackle the problem of faking in proportion to the SDSV of the item by using moderately desirable trait items (Edwards, 1963; 1964b; Puhan & Das, 1980). Their argument, in simple terms, will be, "Don't ask a silly question and you won't get a silly answer". In the rush of modern day living where there is hardly time for establishment of rapport before we start firing the questions having obvious personal implications, this approach seems to be very sensible. But it is sensible merely from a statistical point of view. It is parallel to the concept of

Discriminability as described in Anastasi (1976) for item analysis. The item discriminates the best when moderate difficulty level is chosen in case of ability testing. Kline's (1983) advice of "Generally, if in test construction item writers are careful to avoid obviously socially desirable items and to eliminate items which have extremely unequal response splits, the worst effects of social desirability can be avoided" supports this contention. The contention reflects the inherent conceptual confusion between the SDE as a correlation between the SD score and the trait score and the reaction of actually giving a socially desirable response in the sense of faking. It is very difficult to conceive how statements with high SDSV can ever be written in such a way, at least in the inventory form, that no normal group of persons can give the SD response to it. One needs to be reminded of the impressive agreement among the judges, though admittedly belonging to a particular community (*i.e.*, the ubiquitous university students) when judging the Social Desirability Scale Value of an item. The agreement clearly shows that the SDSV aspect of an item simply stands out (My goodness! Isn't that surprising?). To say that an item can be written, in inventory terms, which will not be susceptible to the SD effect is to make a psychometrically desirable response whose realisation is highly improbable if not impossible. The social desirability aspect of any item must stand out once the so-called neutral area in the social desirability dimension is crossed. More correctly, even in the neutral area the SDSV stands out as being moderate.

Block (1965) suggested item-subtlety as a possible remedy for the SDE. The process uses the items that has very little obvious link with the construct (trait) being studied. This idea thrives on outsmarting the taste-taker in such a way that he would not know what was extracted from him. It is really an attempt to capitalize on the idea that projective tests are resistant to SD effect because the implications of the responses they yield is far from obvious. Such an approach depends a lot on the item writing abilities with a strong dose of intellectual abilities for outsmarting the future test-takers. In the previous chapter, the ridiculous situation in Minsk-Pinsk dilemma has been discussed. Moreover, progressing this way we are quite likely to measure somebody's taste-taking ability rather than the trait itself. Such test-taking abilities will have the person's appreciation of what is socially desirable as a dominant component. It will not tackle SDE. It will serve to send us on a merry-go-round.

From another angle, experimental manipulation through different instructions has been tried to test the resistance of a test. The subjects are instructed to "fake good" or "fake bad". It is expected that depending on the instruction, the subject would try to imitate the response pattern of a great soul or a demented one. If the test scores show no significant variation under these instructions as compared to the alleged normal condition, the test is deemed to be proof against faking. Edwards, in his very first exposition regarding the resistance of the SD microbe to such treatment stated that the SD microbe could well have contaminated the normal score. With the normal sample already containing strains of the microbe, it is hardly likely that the suspected sample would stand out as significantly different. So Edwards (1957) warned against any false sense of well being under such demonstration of resistance on the part of the test. Studies of faking via this method still abound because more often than not the tests show susceptibility to change in line with instructions given.

Edwards's suggested anti-dote involves administration of equally potent poison to take out the suspected poison. In test development terms, it meant balancing each statement with one alternative statement which is scaled to be equally socially desirable or undesirable as the case may be. This was the famous forced-choice format utilized in Edwards' Personal Preference Schedule (Edwards, 1970). A vulgar analogy (after Lumsden, 1976) of the logic behind such a venture would be as follows:

If one wanted to determine whether an individual has the tendency of committing crimes such as rape then he should counter-balance such a self-description with another equally aversive description. Then he should ask the individual to choose one of the two statements as most (or least) descriptive of his dispositions:

A. I always felt I would rape somebody.
B. My feelings run on the line of murdering someone.

Then force the test-taker to choose among the alternatives. It does not matter if the test-taker never felt like doing either. He/she is encouraged to look deep within and come up with something as if life depended on it. The wisdom of such actions, from the point of view of what it aims to achieve can very well be judged. There is very little ground for using the format with moderately desirable (the so-called neutral, subtle, and discriminative) items.

Some psychometricians came up with the excuse that SD is one worrying factor in a selection situation. In a purely academic, non-committal set up of the university research SD effect can safely be forgotten. Kline (1983) takes a somewhat similar line in, "It is also a major reason why it is necessary to have sound evidence that a personality test is valid, because if it is, the question of social desirability becomes otiose" and also in, "The solution used by Edwards (1970) in his own test, the Edwards Personal Preference Schedule (EPPS) was ingenious. He used forced-choice item; the members of each pair from which the choice was made were judged equal in social desirability. However, in our view such elaborate precautions are not necessary unless all validity studies fail"(p. 20).

The problem with such contention is that SD itself is a validity problem. The K, L and F scales of the MMPI are called validity scales and reflect on an individual giving a SD response. On a test level the SD contamination is found by correlating test scores with SD scores. If that is high then other high correlations with so-called validity criterion can only serve to show that SD, rather than the trait, explains the correlation. It is not clear how validity studies, therefore, make the problem of SD otiose. It becomes still unclear when one tries to reconcile the Edwardian demonstration of susceptibility of all the leading inventories to SD and the reporting of validity studies of the inventories thus afflicted at the same time. Secondly, it is difficult to conceptualize what constitute "all validity studies" and "fail" even by conventional standards. There has been no accepted standard implying success or failure in the validity criteria. As pointed out by Mischel, the validity index does not seem to be going higher than .3. If this does not imply failing then what does? It seems, for all practical purposes this contention aims to completely ignore the SD problem. (The author reached the same conclusion but from a different perspective on SD). The way the conclusion is reached even when the virulence of the syndrome is accepted may speak volumes about Kline's love of a worry-free (don't worry-be happy!) good life but certainly comes as cold comfort to them who are still facing the terminal stage.

To prove that he has mastered the SD effect in his inventories, Eysenck & Eysenck (1964) developed one orthogonal (which, as we know, implies no effect) Lie scale. This was the no-nonsense, fire and brimstone breathing Eysenck in his pure elements. No SDs, no apologetics. A person who scores high on Lie scale is, well if it must be said, a liar! A logical conclusion following this no-nonsense approach would be to suggest throwing away the data with higher Lie score on the ground of being prejudicial to our search for truth. However, Eysenck stopped well short of that point. He merely advised caution (whatever that may mean) in using data with high Lie scores. Moreover, he found that it might be indicative, to some extent, of a stable personality factor (How about that?). The Lie score also refused to be as factorially independent as he would have liked it to be. As a compromise, he made lying a group offence. Instead of needing the tester to diagnose somebody as a liar, the suggestion was given to eliminate, in steps of 5%, the data containing high L scores (Eysenck and Eysenck, 1975). One is left to his own ingenuity when working with a single person with a high L score. Need it be emphasized that there are not too many takers of this idea which seemed to have been added as an after-thought to counter the nasty SD which was spoiling the robust beauty of the EPQ.

Somebody came up with the brilliant idea that the SD response mostly implies jacking up of trait scores, having high social desirability connotation. Therefore, some scales like the K scale of MMPI, yielding an index of jacking, can be gainfully used to jack down the individual's score to an ordinary level, bringing the seekers of truth nearer to their cherished goal. To deny the rumour that psychologists cannot accept the fact when people report being really good and cut him to size, it must be mentioned also that psychologists cannot accept when poor soul reports that he is really rotten as well. So they jack him up via K score. For various reasons, such endeavour has not been highly promoted (Anastasi, 1976).

3.3.1. Technological Advancement and the anti-SD Warfare

Now-a-days one expects a computer to do everything. It is hardly surprising that while developing Personal Research Form (PRF) Jackson brought in the computer to tackle the SD effect (Jackson, 1967c; 1970). Anastasi (1976) observed, "with regard to the procedure followed in defining scales and in formulating and selecting items, the PRF is truly outstanding among personality tests" (p. 513). What interests us here is the process through which items were distilled from the SD contamination. Hogan (in Buros, 1980) mentioned that the three criteria followed for item selection were:

(1) Endorsement frequency between 5 and 95%.
(2) High correlation with provisional key for each scale and
(3) Low correlation with social desirability scale.

This was followed by some item-metric refinements. Yet Hogan mentioned : "But many writers after surveying the literature on this topic feel that social desirability represents valid rather than error variance. Purifying the test items at the very beginning has not helped Jackson much, as Hogan observed, "In summary, this is an interesting and marvelously well constructed test whose empirical validity (after ten years) has yet to be demonstrated"(p.1008). Without a clear understanding a powerful method like factor analysis can only serve as a late twentieth century tribal magic to excorcise SD affliction with little result.

Even when these psychometric stalwarts were fighting valiantly they seem to be seeing a different face of SD with regularity.

Somehow, their battle-wary brains took those sightings as apparitions and they avoided making a fuss about it. The manual for PRF mentions that the high or low scores on the desirability scale may imply important personality traits besides dissimulation. Eysenck and Eysenck (1975) also accept this. Crowne and Marlowe (1964) took this aspect seriously and came up with the substantial Need for Approval with its attendant predictability. But while Need for Approval was one among the many desirable needs, SD happened to be almost the one and only among undesirables. So need for approval was replaced by Marlowe-Crowne Desirability scale as an alternative to Edwards SD scale. And thus, the attempt at purifying the test, still goes on.

3.4 How to stop "Faking"

Though SD responding is thought of as unconscious faking, SD and faking or lying has been used synonymously with impunity in the research literature. SD can be understood from a different perspective that would not need any *tackling*. But faking and lying are different matters. The problem of faking can never be tackled operationally. The logic is straightforward. In order that individual differences can be reflected in a test, it should allow at least two alternative responses, such as agree/disagree, true/false etc.. The moment the alternatives come in, all that is required of a subject to fake the test is to give a different response than the one he intended to give. There is simply no way it can be stopped. A logical approach to reveal faking would be to locate inconsistencies in test responses. But these inconsistencies have to be demonstrated using near identical statements. Statements are subject to individual's own interpretations and, therefore, cannot establish the fact that they meant the same thing if they are not identical. The alternative of having identical statements placed in different parts of the test will not be useful. People do remember the items they have already responded to. The repetition of questions would offend them or make them uneasy. Correspondingly, the test-taker would label the questions (More likely, the whole test) as either dumb or having ulterior motives in which case the test-taker is hardly expected to give a 'closer-to-reality' response. Apart from these considerations, such inconsistencies may be due to momentary fluctuations or genuine errors of response. The presence of these alternative interpretations implies that the veracity of a response can only be established with the support and informed consent of the respondent. It brings home to us the fact that rapport needs to be established in every testing situation. It is more so given the general apprehension on the part of psychometricians regarding the numerosity of liars, fakes and SD responders in the population. The actual status of rapport, however, leaves much to be desired.

3.5 On Establishing Rapport

Anastasi (1976) stated, "In psychometrics, the term "rapport" refers to the examiner's efforts to arouse the subject's interest in the test, elicit his cooperation, and ensure that he follows the standard test instructions. In ability tests, the instructions call for careful concentration on the given tasks and putting forth one's best effort to perform well; in personality inventories, they call for frank and honest responses to questions about one's usual behaviour; in certain projective tests, they call for full reporting of associations evoked by the stimuli, without any censoring or editing of content. Still other kinds of tests may require other approaches. But in all instances, the examiner endeavours to motivate the subject to follow the instructions as fully and conscientiously as he can"(p.34).

Establishment of rapport, in inventory research, has become very conspicuous by the absence of any documentation in the test manuals and correspondingly in research articles. It is very difficult to achieve rapport in a group-testing situation. It is true that the huge number of data that feeds the impressive statistical analysis in psychometric research would not have been easy to collect without group testing procedure. Since inventories have been taken (mistakenly) as less amenable to psychological states, establishment of rapport has been given the backseat. Remuneration per hour spent with the test or giving course credit or even the acceptance of the invitation of forming the subject pool for psychological experiments are not insurances against respondent's disenchantment with the process yielding random data. The basic process of rapport built through friendly human interaction can never be replaced. It is the *sine qua non* of the testing process. Any response, if it has to have the authenticity in the majority of the cases, must be elicited with the informed consent of the subject. Trying to hoodwink the subject cannot be allowed to hold central place in the development of tests.

The argument against having elaborate mention of rapport in the test manuals will center on the fact that it is not specific to any particular test. It would be much better if the tests were accompanied by photocopies of Anastasi's (or comparable) advice, to complete the necessary manual. She mentioned various misuses, misconceptions of psychological tests culled from real life incidents. The author himself has taken part in some studies and can vouchsafe that only the love for psychology kept him going through the tests. The data collection procedure described elsewhere highlights the author's feeling about this part of research.

Unfortunately, our love for so-called objectivism and the illusion of producing fake-proof tests is so complete that very few inventory users care to establish rapport with the test- takers. Eysenck's EPQ, in a rather curt manner, advises the test-takers not to think too much and answer the question. It is difficult to justify the reason that expects a person to reveal his awareness of his innermost feelings, and beliefs etc. in the name of research, to a strange practitioner of the barely understood discipline of psychology who seems to have little time to explain himself and his tests! Possibly because the subjects in psychological testing are mostly volunteers in the Western countries, and are obliging students under instruction from their teachers. No wonder, that the nicety or rather the essentiality of establishing rapport is viewed as superfluous. The only way that is both ethical and effective through which one can ever ensure that the subject does give the response he feels like giving is by clarifying the intention, giving sufficient time to think over, understand and feel free to ask questions etc. Somehow the essential requirement of establishing rapport before testing must have reeked of subjectivism to the ultra-behaviouristic psychometricians. Also somebody might have found those little nuisances could not be reduced to numbers (to allow some sort of statistical test of significance to add to the force of one's contention) and hence were not worth the bother. In any case, this led the psychometricians to the unenviable task of eliciting responses almost in spite of rather than with the help of the respondent.

3.6 On Asking Silly Questions

If one asks a silly question then he will get only a silly answer. Sensible questions asked sensibly, provided the person has not already been put off by the silly questions asked earlier, will beget a sensible answer. However, the answer to a silly question cannot be used to determine the authenticity of an answer given to a sensible question.

The items in the Lie and SD scales have one important characteristic in common. They are all very silly. An assorted sample of such items from the EPQ are, "Have you ever taken praise for something you knew someone else had really done?", "As a child did you do as you were told immediately and without grumbling?" etc. Other measurements of SD match the silliness of the L scale. A reference to real life situations would reveal that such questions would not be very acceptable even when put by/to one's close friends. Just because it is put in a test form (in the garb of scientific research) it should not be construed to be essentially any different. It merely serves to expose how far the psychometricians have gone away from 'real life' and towards developing a 'science of test-taking behaviour'.

Apart from this lack of contact with reality, there are ethical considerations as well. It would not be very ethical to make derogatory inferences about a person (being liar, etc.) and giving it a scientific colour without informing the person. On the other hand, if debriefing (as used in experimental social psychology) is routinely carried out to be consistent with the guidelines then, after a decade, psychological tests will be deemed as something to watch out against. Public resentment of the use of psychological tests for selection, etc. has been building up. Such resentment is mostly ignored through our typical holier-than-thou, wise man-in-search-of-truth attitude towards academic research. Such attitudes would be commendable had the logic of the approach been impeccable. The analysis has shown the facts to be different.

3.7. SD and Reality

The SD effect is considered as noxious because psychometricians have felt, for various reasons, that it has kept them at an arm's length from the coveted reality which is unambiguous and unique. A closer look at human experience will reveal that there is no fixed reference point called the reality. For long, realities of hypnotic experience, perceptual defence and sublimation etc. have been rejected in various degrees by academic psychologists as fictions. Rogers (1973) made a valiant attempt to bring the other 'reality' to the notice of psychologists, a reality that they, normally, would know nothing about. It, nevertheless, exists in a person's experience. Hilgard (1980) has also argued for the acceptance of alternative states of consciousness and reality. A rational approach, in view of the not-so-phenomenal success of the so-called objective psychology, would have been to permit the conceptualization of alternative realities. But such contentions have fallen mostly on deaf ears.

It is interesting to note that the idea of one reality in the so-called objective psychology is taken for granted even by persons who have been trying to challenge the monopoly. However, the logic and the evidence as evinced from research findings do merit a different conclusion. Not only are there as many realities as there are persons involved in experiencing, directly or indirectly, but also there are at least three realities for each human experience. These realities pertain to the three aspects namely the cognitive, the affective, and the conative. Though emphasizing on different aspect has waxed and waned with the latest fad in research, no primacy of control for any single aspect has ever been established. Recent research into the relationship among these aspects has yielded contradictory evidence depending on the theoretical standpoint of the researchers. Some found that cognition determines the affective tone of our experiences (Mandler,1982; Weiner,1982). In contrast, Zajonc (1980) felt that affect determines cognition. Roger's (1981) study could not clarify the relationship of cognition with overt behaviour. But, Berkowitz (1983) demonstrated the role of affect in determining aggression. Kiesler (1982) suggested that the relationship of cognition and affect will be the core theoretical problem for the coming years. But any conclusion that can be drawn now certainly precludes any ascription of ascendancy to any particular aspect of human experience over the other. Be that as it may, a little getting away from the sheer force of intellectual exercise (the process of academic research) might help in making the author's contention clear which is as follows:

If, for example, a person states that he is sorry, feels happy and yet, shows the signs of dejection, there is nothing in the world which can enable us to ascertain which is the only reality. Depending on the situation we ascribe ascendancy to different aspect in day-to-day living conditions. But, such ascription is absolutely a matter of convenience, not based on any solid proof. Even if the person cooperates with the researcher the person will carry his own bias regarding what his true state was. If this example seems far-fetched then the subsequent example will show how society encourages a dichotomy, if not the trichotomy, of our experience. Possibly that is why so much regard is given to self-actualized persons whose three aspects of experience function in harmony (Maslow, 1965). Unfortunately, there are so few of that kind that we study them as a separate speci rather than as a randon sample. The way a child gets socialized, learns the rules of behaviour to be shown on various social occasions, must shape the unity or diversity of the aspects of experience. A major part of being socialized lies in being polite and respecting others' feelings, etc. These nice aspects of being civilized have their own shortcomings. A child learns to negate the feelings *i.e.*, to say 'very nice' when he feels 'sick' or 'disgusted'. Civilized adults do so as well. One striking experience, in England, revealed to me how far this 'being civilized' can be stretched. A friend of mine who used to give me lift to the university was served 'a quick cup of tea'. I had put two tea-bags in a cup to make it quick but forgot to take those out quickly as well. Learning to be civilized the British way, I asked if it was okay. And after sipping he said, "It is okay" (!) When I came back to have my tea, I found it to be undrinkable. When I asked him about his tea, he was a bit hesitant but still said, "Honestly (!), it is okay". Being less civilized (and stronger as well) than he was, I simply snatched his cup away and poured it in the washbasin. Over a cup of regularly made Indian tea, I asked how he could torture himself like that. He just smiled. (How's that as research data?)

In case it is construed that the so-called instinctive reaction (bereft of cognitive connotations) to a situation is the true reality, it must be emphasized that human beings are blessed with cognition and much more power lies in the mind and brain than we care to give it. A man can get physically hungry, scared and yet use his will-power or cognition to take his thoughts away from these aspects so much that he can manage to control and regulate his behaviour without feeling under pressure. It is funny that psychologists are in constant need of being reminded that cognition is quite powerful and can create as much a reality of its own as affection and overt behaviour can.

The same can be said of overt behaviour. Unlike the Wild West movies, in which the macho hero never speaks, much less shows his emotions, everybody expects the physical and external posture to convey the reality of love, hate, and anger etc. Many rightly would feel that it is not enough to say or feel but to show. An oft-quoted statement is, "Justice must not only be administered but also appear to have been administered." One can easily discern the importance given to the appearance in any society.

As a group of social animals intelligibly communicating with each other, we have never been consistent in our ascription of importance to the different aspects. Often, when we hate someone, we denigrate a good demonstrated behaviour as false covering up bad intentions and feelings. Equally often, we defend bad expressions if they are followed by good action. It all seems to be dependent on the time and the perceiver and, therefore, so whimsical. As a group of researchers, we have fared no better. There is no consensus on what aspect of our lives constitute a greater reality even from the limited 'researcher' point of view.

Some feel that physiological measurements constitute a more real down-to-earth reality than do the mumbo-jumbo world of psychological measurement. By their logic, modern sophisticated polygraphs could identify "lying" better than the Lie scales in the psychological tests. The fact is those instruments merely record the relevant physiological changes as they occur in the human body. They do not identify the unique presence of lying. Only when the subject cooperates, physiological changes corresponding to verbally reported "lying" could be recorded. But that does not imply that these recorded changes uniquely define the existence of lying. In fact, a lot of brainwashing of the subject using psychological principle takes place before the polygraph is used as lie detectors. Still they fail (Orne *et. al.*, 1972). It must be emphasized that lying, in legal sense of denying any specific knowledge of acts of omission or commission, is very different from the sense in which it is used in the Social Desirability context.

3.8. Meehl's Faking & Jourard's Confessions

Meehl & Hathaway (1946) were worried about "unconscious self-deception" and "role-playing" on the part of the subjects who may, in general, be quite "honest" and sincere in their responses to the personality statements contained in the personality inventories." That portrayed the discomfiture of psychometricians who felt that something was going wrong and yet they were not able to pin down the fault or the guilty party involved. Here two observations can be made. Hartshorne & May (1928; 1929), after conducting a series of studies, failed to locate an unchanging structure of honesty as a trait. Some psychologists later analyzed the data and found a "factor" of honesty but that hardly established honesty as an unvarying trait. It helped to explain why 'otherwise quite honest' persons would fake the inventories. The other point is that self-deception and role-playing are two words used almost synonymously in that context. The previous discussion has shown that "deception" cannot be established because the reality of "self" is far from clear. In fact, along with role-playing, self-deception is the process by which we conquer our instincts and become socialized and civilized human beings. The author finds the concept of a life beyond the role-playing of a father, a friend, a teacher, and, in the spare time (which is rare), a human being, is very hard if not impossible to conceptualize. For the majority of us, life carries the meaning as long as it relates to our social life. Each of the different aspect of social life has as much salience as we care to give it through our self-concept and the social exigencies. If my self-concept includes 'a caring father' my behaviour will vary along that line more than it would on the dimension of extraversion-introversion as defined by Eysenck. We do not even notice the change of role as it seems to be gently fading into the other. On this point, we do not feel to be living a self-deceiving life. We are quite happy to find some uniformity amidst diversity in human life through role-playing.

It is interesting to note Jourard's (1979) self-analysis regarding this. He stated, "I pondered how one would do research into the process of being one's real self in relation to others. I thought it was a question of telling others the truth, and letting other people know you. Then, I wondered, "who knows me?" I asked members of my family, friends and colleagues to tell what they know of me. Their answers were so diverse that I hardly recognized the person they were describing. I wondered how they got those impressions of me, and realized I played an important part in determining how well any other person knew me. In fact, there was much about me I did not want others to know. Much of my action was aimed at misleading others, at misinforming them about the person I knew myself to be"(p.1). The author feels that such self-confessions are misleading as it tends to suggest that there is one real self in every human being. In real terms, the studies Jourard referred to, far from locating that one real self, merely highlighted self-disclosure, exposure of one's ideas, feelings, perceptions that were dominant at any particular time but were found undesirable at that time. This is distinctly different from what is implied in the above-mentioned paragraph. There are many more realities for any person than one. Often, even the person himself may not know what is the reality for him. The essentially multidimensional nature cannot be tackled by using self-confessions of a highly obliging subject.

Koch (1981) in an incisive article wrote, "Consider now the enormous ranges of inherent ambiguity in the human conditions suggested by, say, the unrecoverability of particular motives and, indeed, the principled impossibility of achieving a full motivational analysis of any actions; the ubiquitous problem of self-sincerity, altruism versus egocentrism, guilt versus innocence, sinful versus good deeds, personal responsibility versus shaping or control from without; of whether, in particular instances or in general, one is loved or hated, liked or disliked, or perhaps regarded indifferently; whether one is beautiful or ugly or somewhere in between"(p.263). Among the many examples cited one was, 'Do I really understand this equation, this line of poetry or prose, this view, theory, subject, person, event?' Do I really like (*e.g.*, any object of tests) or only think that I do because I should? As a matter of fact, 'Should I, really?' 'Should I wear X or Y today or are they both inappropriate?' 'Am I showing favoritism towards one of my children, or is that child the one who needs special attention?'(p. 264).

Koch has shown a far better insight into the opposing dimensions in human life, all of which have equal reality. He mentioned that such ambiguity is the basis of the need of human being's cognitive endeavour to employ conceptual boxes. While this might be the only thing to do to escape the sheer indeterminacy of psychological explanations, controversies and opposing views make us aware of the other dimensions. Surprisingly, while alternative interpretations abound in other areas of psychology the grand SD concept never seems to have been seriously challenged in psychometrics though it is based on a flimsy ground. It seems to thrive on a general disbelief of the respondents by the psychometrician who have managed to make a science of a prejudice.

3.9. Do People Behave in a Socially Desirable Way?

Whether people are necessarily good or bad is not a question the author is trying to solve. The contention is merely that human beings are social beings and spend a lot of time learning what is socially desirable and behave accordingly which has sustained society till the present day. These may be, in some cases, due to internalized super-ego, in others the fear of punishment, or expectancy of reinforcement, in yet some others an essential goodness of human beings. It is undesirable behaviour which makes the news and thereby creates the impression of imminent doom (Latane & Darley, 1968). It is worthwhile to mention that after the 'Crime Watch' program on BBC television, which provides rather vivid details of the crimes committed with the hope that some viewers might come up with helpful tips, the comperes always reassure the viewers that such matters are really very rare. It is time to reassure the psychometricians that there are more persons behaving in socially desirable way than are given respect for.

The previous discussions have exposed the sheer futility of the exercises aiming to tackle SD as an indicator of faking or lying. A reconceptualization of the SD effect and its efficacy would provide the necessary respite to the harassed test developers along the inventory or semi-inventory (like the PI) lines. It will also provide an essential bridge between the findings in social and personality psychology.

A Reconceptualization

3.10. What is Social about Social Desirability?

As has been elaborated in the previous chapter, in the process of socialization, a child is always taught moderation, to avoid too much of anything however nice that thing may seem to be. Even in the achievement sphere there are parents who are opposed to "straining" their high-achieving offspring for various reasons. Right or wrong, moderation is supported in the society. Genetic predisposition, and the reinforcement contingencies used in socialization processes determine where in the dimension a particular person finds his dynamic equilibrium. This balance is maintained more or less through out one's lifetime unless some personal experience changes it. From this point of view, all extremes, considered in abstraction as traits, are to be deemed as socially undesirable, which include being very honest, very pious, and very humble, etc. No matter what trait the item purports to measure, it is coloured by social norms and desirabilities. Society and its desirabilities (SD) have very big roles to play in shaping the various traits. It is only when traits are deemed as innate and genetically determined bereft of any social influence that SD effect can be seen as undesirable.

Edwards (1957) was not talking about any social behaviour but about some aspects of the responses given to test items. This was unfortunately named social desirability that actually implied unconscious faking. He conveniently made the SD scale a rational one without the need to show empirical support (Edwards, 1970). Combined with that, the attitude of "Of course, there are some persons who had never told a lie, never hurt a fly but what about the others?" has provided a can't-lose situation for Edwards. If one makes rather libelous supposition that most of the test-takers fake unconsciously (another convenient supposition) then it better have some solid evidence. After more than forty years of the discovery of the social desirability effect, there is no excuse for not providing any evidence. It is no point gainsaying that nobody asked for it. The logic that creates a kind of special class of tests called rational tests (*e.g.*, SD is the one and only known) without any need to refer to reality is psychologically indefensible.

It is not at all a difficult thing to devise a situation for observation where the social desirability of the situation determining the behaviour can be studied. The problem of SD as studied by Edwards is an artifact of the test items and a rigid conceptualization of the traits. The statements in an inventory highlight only one dimension as per the pet theory of the test-developer. There is no context specified on which to base one's decision. Life is never bereft of context. When put in a social context, moderation seems to be the desirable behaviour. The majority supports no extreme behaviour. What is moderate is socially desirable, if seen from the right perspective.

Edward's demonstration of the super high agreement using some extreme statements is contrary to what is experienced in life. But it can easily be explained. If the raters agreed that a yes response to a question like "I have never told a lie" means extreme social desirability then it is because the behaviour is taken out of its context. People lie for a host of reasons not the least of which is for being polite! In a highly formalized society like the British society, the number of times people qualify their observation with 'honestly' (and possibly still be dishonest!) shows the importance of context. Without the context, a civilized nation can be labeled as a nation of liars! Just because Marks & Spencers reports a loss of some million pound sterling on account of pilferaging per year, one cannot label the Britishers as a nation of shop-lifters (shop-keepers may be alright, to some extent, honestly!) So, context must be there in social life and it should not be any different in psychometrics. There will never be any show of the impressive agreement when context is put firmly in its deserving place. This merely would reflect that, in reality, disagreement is more the rule than exception. It is imperative that the context be brought back into the testing situation if we are to talk about a human social behaviour rather than human test-taking behaviour.

Edwards (1969) made a long-winded analysis of 90 trait names for studying evaluative consistency. Then some judges were given the trait names to evaluate the similarity between the items. The task was to judge the characteristic of a person as 'timid' or 'bold' from the description of he being 'cautious' or 'rash' etc. Then some other people were asked to describe themselves. Edwards was impressed that while judges chose the terms to be cautious and timid the self-description went somewhat on 'cautious and bold' lines. That provided Edwards with another example of lying. But such an outcome can perfectly logically be expected if the context is brought back into the picture. It has been argued repeatedly that every individual uniquely determines the dynamic resolution of the opposing force conflict. When he decides to go in any direction there is always the opposing force which pushes him back. Once the individual takes a decision, he usually shuts his eyes to the existence of the other dimension. Otherwise he would never find any equilibrium. As far as the individual himself is concerned he is just 'cautious' and definitely not 'timid'! How many introverts would have continued to be so if they were told that they were conceited and egocentric? And for that matter how many would have remained extraverts if they were told that they were positive nuisances and show-offs? It is only when a judge is asked without being told the context that he sees both the dimensions with such semantic clarity. Socially, such clarity is very rare. Such studies do not demonstrate a kind of general lying syndrome but indicate the way different individuals construe the behaviour in the presence and absence of context.

Another misleading piece of research is the development of a likeableness scale of 555 trait terns (Anderson, 1968). The same error of taking away the context applies here. Apparently, honesty would be more desirable than extraversion. But if we juxtapose the traits with the context put in such as "I will be honest even if that means hurting some innocent persons" and "I would go to a party even if I had exam the next morning" the likeableness rating is not going to hold good. The situation would not be substantially improved if some kind of subtraction value for social undesirability from the scale were used. It is the absence of context which has created the SD effect serving to bedevil the efforts of trait psychologists.

3.11. Law of Parsimony and the SD

The law of parsimony holds that if a phenomenon is completely described by alternative theories or factors then, the one which uses less number of suppositions or variables is to be deemed as the best under the circumstances. Edwards had done a lot of factor analyses which showed that SD score had extremely high loading on the first factor on which most of the tests also loaded highly. So — under the law of parsimony he insisted that instead of using so many different tests under so many different trait names, one should parsimoniously use one SD scale. However, as has been mentioned before, no one has tried to use the SD scale to predict various differences in the trait scores either at the group or at the individual level.

But as Edwards himself has stated it is not a trait but an aspect of the trait statements. In fact, he (1970, p. 232) mentioned about each trait items can be scaled for dimensions of health-sickness, adjustment-maladjustment and normality-abnormality etc. and that it might correlate highly with rates of SD responding.

Apart from the fact that it is the artifact of the testing situation, there are psychological explanations of why SD cannot replace every trait scale. It merely points out the social roots of all our behaviours (from which traits are inferred). Similar to the futility of reducing all kinds of behaviour to the action of muscles and glandular secretion for greater objectivity, the futility of reducing all behaviour as fundamentally social in nature should be realised without further delay. It cannot reveal how an individual's behaviour differs from others having same social desirability. It might help in prediction of how many persons would say 'yeah' or 'nay' but it will not greatly improve one's understanding of such processes.

From the statistical point of view, no matter how impressive factor loading may look, there is still a lot of variance left to be explained even in Edwards's studies. There is also the problem of explaining unique variance that is never highlighted. There are so many ifs and buts in factor analysis that it cannot be used to contend for the application of law of parsimony. Of course, another interesting thing about psychological research is that no matter what kind of evidence is put against a test, the proponents go on peddling their wares with gay abandon. Edwards's efforts at exposing the (till now well established) limitations have not stopped others from using the well-known tests. (It is only the new-comers like the PIAPEN which have to face the difficulty). A closer analysis of Edwards's forced-choice method advocated in his EPPS reveals interesting aspects. The respondent is encouraged to choose as most/least descriptive of him between a pair of items, an example of which is as follows :

(A) I like to talk about myself to others.
(B) I like to work towards some goal that I have set for myself.

The two items were matched for their Social Desirability Scale Values. Edwards (1959) mentioned that some subjects *seem to resent the forced-choice.* Every individual must make a choice in the day-to-day living, between the opposing forces. It is only when the alternatives are seen as non-exclusive that leads to irritation. Both the alternatives used in the EPPS could be descriptive of one-self or equally non-descriptive. There does not seem to be any actual opposition between them except for the item format itself. This will always be the case in the traditional approach because the context is never allowed to play an important role. In any case, the EPPS only yielded ipsative scores that while providing some new information cannot be expected to replace the traditional inventory approach. The opposed forces idea is rather more gainfully applied in the PI approach because each judgement has a reference with the context firmly put in to be referred to as many times as required by the respondent. (The details are described in the method chapter).

3.12 In a Nutshell

It is only fair to mention again that the PI method was initially created to tackle the SD effect on the misleading notion that projective tests are not susceptible to that effect. In fact, the influence of the conventional approach to SD made outsmarting of the test-takers good fun and stimulating. Then gradually, as the realization regarding the true nature of SD dawned, a drastic change in approach took shape. The pervasiveness of the SD effect served to refine the research ideas, but it was found to have no bearing on the subsequent research design in establishing the efficiency of the PI as a method of testing personality.

"I am afraid I cannot put it more clearly", Alice replied, very politely, "for I can't understand it myself, to begin with: and being so many different sizes in a day is very confusing."

Four

On Reliability and Validity of Tests

4. Introduction

Whoever has heard of test reliability and validity being discussed even before the test is developed? Even though the traditional viewpoint treats them with reverence as benchmarks of test efficacy, they have their places in the ordering, which comes much later in test development. The steps for a test-developer are apparently well laid out (*e.g.*, Kline, 1983; Nunnally, 1978), which could be as follows: Define the traits, write down the items, analyze the items for elimination and then study the reliability and validity of a test. In fact, so good was (and still is by the look of it) the established convention that it provided a happy hunting ground for copious output in the form of developed tests as witnessed in the Mental Measurement Yearbooks. For all practical purposes, beyond some petty family squabbles such as the SD effect, it has been one big happy and healthy family of tests.

But, to the discerning, there has been signs of insidious growth of discontentment against the regimentation. It needs careful study. The very basic concepts and their utility are being challenged. So, we need to put the point in right perspective. Anastasi, one of the leading authorities on test development stated in 1976, "Reliability of a test refers to the consistency of scores obtained by the same persons when reexamined with the same test on different occasions or with different sets of equivalent items, or under other variable examining conditions" (p.103). She further stated, "Validity of a test concerns what the test measures and how well it does it" (p.134). These descriptions of the concepts acknowledge the complexity involved in the processes. Beyond that, the different ways through which the reliability and validity co-efficients could be calculated are also dealt with at length. And yet, nowhere in the detailed analysis, the efficacy of the processes involved was doubted. No matter what the complexity involved was, a test needed to have some indices of reliability and validity.

Between them, validity is acknowledged as more important of the two concepts because it seems to be closely related to the 'truth' rather than the 'true score'. But, since the calculation process afforded limited sophistication involved in playing around with numbers and the ambiguity of the work involved, validity studies have played second fiddle to reliability studies. For a comparison, the validity indices never seemed to go beyond .30 which brought derision from Mischel (1968) as the limit of "personality co-efficient" whereas reliability indices always seemed to be soaring around .80 level. Under Goebbel's principle of repeating a falsehood many times (consistently) to establish authenticity, psychometricians decided to measure whatever they seemed to measure consistently without bothering to know what it was that they were measuring. An example of this is Jackson's PRF deemed by many as the epitome of technical efficiency but, as Hogan (1980) pointed out, after ten years of whose existence, any relationship with life outside has not been demonstrated. Such ideas also led many to insist that a test must be reliable before it can be valid. In fact, the reliability coefficient is taken to be defining the highest limit of validity indices. The only dissenting voice seems to have come from Cattell and Kline (1977). But mostly, there has been slavish following of the recommended steps and the test developer felt his job well done and completed once such criteria were met.

Such a state of affairs has given rise to persistent attacks on the psychometric monoliths of reliability (Bock & Wood, 1971; Lumsden, 1976, 1977, 1978) and validity (Fitzpatrick, 1983; Fiske, 1973, 1976; Lumsden, 1976) over the years. Lumsden minced no words when he put across the psychometricians the futility of the very fundamental concepts of reliability and the 'true score' on which it is based. Very few articles have been written with that kind of venom. It must have come out of a genuine concern for the lack of growth of understanding in the area and the beating around the bush that goes on in the name of academics. Even though almost all the leading psychometricians who peddled their wares were ruthlessly exposed, no one has been able to give an adequate reply, so far. There is also no reason to feel that any would be forthcoming. On that strength alone, he has left the monoliths, if not crumbling, in a state of acute disrepair. This chapter will highlight the salient points.

Reliability

4.1. The Concept

Before analyzing the assaults on it, it is worthwhile to understand the nature of the sustenance of reliability and validity as psychometric concepts and why they have proved to be so much resistant to attacks even when all their logical supports have apparently vanished. In our constant aping of sciences, our measurement found an ideal in the area of instrumentation in Physics. Reliability as a concept developed analogous to the concept of precision in instrumentation. All other things remaining constant, the fact of an instrument yielding more or less the same value over repeated measurements referred to the reliability of the test. Precision stands for greater sophistication and higher degree of accuracy as a result of the technological advancement. Since a precision instrument is taken as reliable, it was accepted as essential for the development and proper use of tests.

4.1.1. The Limitations

There have been some very basic differences between the two concepts from the very beginning. The fact that there existed (still exists) various methods of testing reliability *viz.* Test-retest, Split-half, Kuder-Richardson Formula 20 (KR-20), and Alternate/Parallel-form, etc. clearly indicated that reliability is not a unitary concept as precision. As per the very definition of Reliability, it refers to the correlation between the two sets of scores yielded by two separate administrations of the same test with an optimum time gap. But since psychometricians never actually got down to agree on the optimum time gap, and the fact that subject attrition, and practice and boredom effect cannot be avoided, alternative methods of testing reliability were sought for. The enterprising brains devised the Split-half and the Spearman-Brown prophecy formula to circumvent the problem. Split-half procedure allowed a simulation of two administrations by splitting a test into two halves. The correlation between the two halves was suitably increased *via* the prophecy formula. This increment was based on the statistical logic of: 'other things being equal' a longer test would yield greater reliability score than a shorter one. Though the first step looks innocuous, it poses one of the most difficult tasks. A test could contain odd number of items. As in a personality test, the items are not comparable to each other as they do not refer to the same traits. One simply cannot split these tests into any two meaningfully comparable halves. Regarding the use of the prophecy formula, Lumsden (1976) pointed out that there is no empirical proof that the prophecy based on the assumption that (again all things remaining constant) a longer test is more reliable (and, therefore, more valid) than a shorter one, is true. Theoretically, there is nothing special about it. Any equation with diminishing return with an asymptote of 1.00 would do the job as well. Moreover, Bell and Lumsden (1980) empirically demonstrated that the prophecy does not work in the validity context and that a test can be reduced by 60%, saving a lot of time and effort, without any noticeable reduction of predictive validity. They also advocated that the tests should undergo such routine checks to locate what proportion of the tests could be reduced. There is no reason to believe that it will be completely different with reliability. Lumsden (1976) used 'vulgar analogy', a potent device to make things clearer, in his article. Using the same device, we can try to understand the process as comparable to the following: Suppose that we want to know whether a person is maintaining constant weight over a period of time. But, at the same time, we have a nagging doubt about his coming for the second time for the check up. For the sake of science, will it be credible to cut him in two and weigh the two parts to simulate the second administration and to infer about the weight consistency?

Proponents of parallel-form reliability were not happy with the reduction in the reliability index in case of the split-half approach. So, in their sincerity, they developed tests on the basis that the tests producing comparable total scores for the same individual are technically the same and can be used interchangeably. This approach could take care of the dreaded practice and fatigue variables that were confounding the results of test-retest reliability. It could also take care of the subject attrition and the optimum time gap problem. But, it can still be debated whether parallel-form reliability demonstrates the reliability of the tests or merely how parallel the parallel-form is to the original test. If we are to use 'vulgar analogy' using the example given for measuring weight consistency in the previous paragraph, instead of cutting the person in two, we can use the person's sibling or even a close friend, or may be his look-alike to test the weight consistency of the person. Wouldn't that be ingenious?

Possibly the most convenient method employed is the Kuder and Richardson (1937) formula. This formula, keeping the lack of unanimity in accepting a particular way for splitting a test in two, advocates the use of the average of all possible combinations of splitting as a better alternative than the split half method. Collected from a single administration of a test, it required that the items to be scored dichotomously. Cronbach's (1951) "Co-efficient alpha" evolved to take multiple-choice items into consideration on Kuder-Richardson's lines. Except for Kline and Cattell (1977), most test developers agree that KR-20 is essential for higher validity. But, critically analysed, it merely demonstrates which of the items group together from the subjects' viewpoint, on an average. It speaks nothing about the consistency of the scores across time and space. It is difficult to comprehend how one can comprehend the average of all possible split-halves when it is almost impossible to comprehend a meaningful split-half done even once. (Is that why talk about three kind of lies: Lies, damned lies and statistics?)

When we take each of the methods of calculating the reliability indices individually, it is not difficult to see the difficulty involved in the calculation and comprehension. When they are evaluated together, things become worse. How do we determine which of the reliability indices is to be given greater consideration over other, knowing well that they would differ in magnitude (and, God forbid, in direction).

Thus the precision indiccs have become imprecise even in their relationship with each other. There were at least as many reliabilities as there were ways to measure the concept. In addition, the fact that the reliability estimates, even when using the same method, fluctuate from sample to sample, shows that we are playing a different game in Psychology than the people developing precision instruments in Physics. Somehow, the decision of testing the test rather than our conceptualization was so authoritative that consistency of test scores across time and space indicated by a reliability index was hardly ever challenged. Anastasi's (1976) analysis of sources of error variances resulting from time sampling, content sampling and the suggestion of finding true variance by deducting the error variance of a test from unity, has not found many takers for serious test development purposes. It merely provided academic respectability to the wild goose chase of a reliable test.

4.1.2 Error of Measurement (Judgement?)

The standard error of measurement (SEM) is the complimentary concept of reliability and complements it as an index of unclear thinking. There are many adherents of this great idea, which believes in building a different line of defence (called confidence intervals) on both the sides of the true score. Translated to real life, it means the test psychologists should say something like, "Well, it looks like you have a score of 125 but, believe me, it could well be anything from 100 to 150 two third of the times, from 75 to 175 95% of the times and almost certainly between 50 to 200 if you take the test a hundred times." Beyond impressing ourselves with numbers, this is in no way furthering our understanding of human behaviour. Apparently, that was thought to be enough to cater to the concept of human dynamism (or to protect us from legal complications?). But, curiously, in a normative study, which all the psychometricians support, these very same persons would merrily use the observed score of a test as nothing less than the fact. We put in so much of confidence in the test and its administration that we do not talk about the (confidence) intervals. There is nothing wrong in treating the observed score as a fact. What is wrong is that unnecessary rigmarole of statistics makes heavy weather of a simple calculation. We necessarily make a test developer go through unnecessary hardships to yield useless indices. Following Shakespeare one can ask, "if something is not worth doing, is it worth doing it well?"

Beyond the confidence interval, the SEM index of a test being constant, it can never be put to worthwhile use in differential prediction. For a group of scores, the relative positions of individual scores will remain the same no matter which confidence interval we use. For example, if Tom, Dick and Harry score 13, 14 and 15, respectively, on a test having the SEM of 2, there is no way (granting that the scores are not error scores). Harry could be denied the selection in favour of either Tom or Dick on the ground that the test has a high SEM. For all practical purposes the test scores are treated as fixed and most representative of a person's performance as well. No true score estimates or drawing of confidence intervals has really changed that. Barring their entertainment value, these intellectual gimmicks have less use in studying individual differences and in practical applications. One would expect that this precision index be used to compare two similar tests. But the SEM had not been used to compare one test against another to establish supremacy of precision. This imprecise thinking combined with potent doses of statistico-mathematical terminology by the test theorists with less concern about reality have muddled the water still further.

When two administrations of the same test yield two different sets of scores, it is taken to refer to the unreliability of the test. Very few bothered about the true nature of these differences. Cronbach *et. al.* (1972) tried to tackle the problem through G and D studies. For them a test score became not merely the product of test items but it became a product of when, what, where, who and on whom etc. of the test. In other words a test score is deemed as the end product of a process which is affected by many independent variables such as, (1) The tester, (2) the place in which the test takes place, (3) the test-takers, (4) instructions given, and (5) method, etc. Accepting all these as confounding variables from which the precision of the test is to be extracted, Cronbach *et. al.* devised explicit studies which very few had tried to carry out because it was such a long winded-affair. Even if somebody does go through the process, it will not make him any wiser. By no means, the list of variables given as affecting the inventory scores are exhaustive. It is quite likely that the number of persons who take the tests in one session (example of diffusion of responsibility), size of the testing room (claustrophobia), dress of the tester (aesthetic surroundings) etc. can all have some amount of variance to explain. After explaining those variance, one has to handle the task of explaining the variances of those variances across different samples. Therefore, even those who keep the G and D studies in high regard never really bother to carry those out.

4.1.3 Some Theoretical Issues

The whole theoretical structure of reliability draws heavily on the concept of true score. The true score theory assumes that,

(1) An observed score consists of true score and error score, (2) The true scores and error scores are uncorrelated, and (3) A set of error scores is uncorrelated with another set of error scores. The model has got intrinsic simplicity and an apparent reference to reality that has made it into an ideal model.

While others have doubted the use of true score and reliability in tests, Lumsden (1976) showed how indefensible those concepts have been. As mentioned earlier, nobody has ventured to counter his attacks, so far. Unfortunately, this has not been translated into general acceptance of his criticisms. The change in attitude that should have followed the article is nowhere to be seen. For the uninitiated, a few of his mathematical arguments and scathing remarks are sampled below.

4.1.3.1. The Error Component of True Score

The true score theory states: $X_O = X_T + X_E$ which means any Observed score (X_O) is the sum of a True score (X_T) and an Error score (X_E). The True score was conceived as the purest score having no correlation with the ubiquitous, unavoidable and pugnacious error score. In real life, any observed score cannot perfectly estimate the true score because it contains an error score. However, the error scores, being random, would cancel each other out and lead the researcher to the true score (by computing the average) if sufficient number of observations are made. Modeled after the physical measurements where the dimensions are continuous and unlimited, these contentions have inherent limitations while used on an essentially limited psychological measurement. For example, it can easily be seen that a person having high true score can have error scores that are either negative or zero since the highest observed score is fixed for a test. Similarly, persons having low true scores, in comparison, could have error scores which could either be positive or zero. This constraint demonstrates that the true score and error score are not as uncorrelated as initially assumed. That leaves us with the embarrassing fact that the great true score is in error. Cronbach *et. al.* (1972) did raise some points saying that there seemed to be a general tendency for the ascription of a kind of eye-of-god reality to the true score. Unfortunately even Cronbach *et. al.* fell into the same trap of as they were not willing to let go of the concept.

To save grace, Lord and Novick (1968) defined true score as the expected value of the obtained value over replications. From the ideal, eye-of-god-reality, true score came down to down-to-earth reality in the sense that however high one's score is in one observation, the expected value will remain less than the highest possible and the hypothesis that the average error score will be zero. It is empirical and circumvents the problem faced in the previous conception of true score. But, as Lumsden pointed out, "While the expected value of the error score is constant (zero) for all values of T, the variance of error scores is not constant but clearly zero at the maximum and minimum scores and rising to the maximum at a middle value of T. It should be noted also that the distribution of error score is likely to be highly skewed for extreme values of true score because of the bound on obtained score. The break down of homoscedasticity for the bivariate distribution of true and error scores has been demonstrated by Lord (53) (p.255)" He, subsequently, exposed how the assumption of linearity of regression of obtained score on true score is violated by the demonstration of non-linearity of regression of true score on the observed score. This fact is, interestingly, conceded to by Lord and Novick (1968) in a later section.

Finding a nice opening, Cronbach et al (1972) tried to peddle their universe score, "the ideal datum on which to base...decision" (p.15). In their attempt to alleviate the fear of true score, they, in fact, managed to replace it with another score having similar characteristics. As described by them, normal mortals would have to remain content with an estimate of the universe score, which happens to be a linear function of the observed score. Such mathematical acrobatics, coupled with unclear thinking that made a virtue of unnecessary computations, made Lumsden explode, "Let me make this matter painfully obvious with some brilliant mathematics. Suppose that you were unhappily calculating X from Y using some complicated function such as X=AY+B and that someone told you that a better procedure was to calculate

X from Z using the function X = CZ+D. You inquire how to find the Z's and are told that you can estimate these accurately enough from Y using the function Z=EY+F. Would you tell this Drongo[2] to go jump in a polykay, nick himself with a jack knife, or lose himself in a Bayesian revolution?" (p.259-60). Footnote 2 of the article at page 260 read, "Drongo: an extinct Australian bird that slept with it's eyes open and flew with its eyes shut." This admittedly was related to ability and achievement scores but it has to be a real incorrigible zealot supporting the true score to contend that it is different in personality research.

Lumsden ended his attack as, "The conclusion is obvious but I will state in anyway. Reliability theory in its present form should be abandoned. To echo Bock and Wood (7), there seems no point in further prolonging the lives of the true score or the reliability co-efficient, classically defined, as concept in test theory. The problems of reliability should be assimilated into validity and scaling theory where they have already been partly solved. Nothing in this recommendation should be taken as advising students of practice, transfer, or training effects on test scores against calculating test-retest or between form co-efficients. These co-efficients should not, in my opinion, be called reliability co-efficients, but if they are, care should be taken that they are not confused with reliability co-efficient as classically defined". He quotes Shakespeare to add poetry to the academic massacre.

> Macbeth : " ....this is a tale
> Told by an idiot, full of sound and fury,
> Signifying nothing" (p.269).

4.1.4. Why Reliability?

Lumsden analyzed the potential utility of reliability in test development into : (1) To guide test selection, (2) To support inferences about test scores based on regression estimates of true scores and standard error of measurement, and (3) To support inferences about the validity of perfectly reliable tests (correction for attenuation). The first consideration, as has been pointed out, hardly matters in psychology. Everybody peddles his own tests and the reliability index has never featured as an important criterion for test selection on the part of a prospective user. The second is hardly of any use because the raw scores and the regression estimate on the criterion serve equally well. The fact that a correction for attenuation yields a correlation over unity should be enough to stop persons from further engaging in these ventures. Lumsden gives all the detailed mathematical analysis of the shortcomings. Except for boosting the morale and possibly the ego of the test developer, an increased reliability, through correction for attenuation, does little to our understanding of its relationship with external behavior. We truly do not need a test reliability.

4.1.5 Consistency of Persons or Reliability of Tests?

The idea of a true score had a very useful ally in the idea of a trait as fixed. It was thought that if the confounding environment (including all temporary and fluctuating things) could be controlled, identified and isolated then one could get the pure 24 carat trait out in full glory and that such trait score would lead to perfect prediction. The underlying contention seems to be: a test score should not change because the indicated trait does not change. So, if a test score does change then it must be due to error (euphemism for ignorance). Though nobody explicitly took such a stance, it is difficult to visualize anyone supporting a true score idea who does not believe in the fixity of traits, logically and conceptually.

These fluctuations of scores can be seen as individuals dynamically adapting to the apparently same situation *i.e.* the test. Everybody accepts that the same physical situation can be construed differently by the same person on different occasions. It is all part of the dynamic process of adaptation. There is no error because there is no fixed true score. In an essentially dynamic mechanism, we are wrong in looking for a rigid true score and feeling bad that it could not be discovered. An essentially wrong reasoning led to wasting of time in solving a problem that should not have been there. Reliability as distinct from validity was wrongly conceptualized and we have paid the penalty. The approach taken up by author does not constitute a convenient escape from the great problem of reliability under Lumsden's banner but it capitalizes on his mathematics and uses psychological and logical analysis to provide an alternative system which integrates itself into the so-called problems of validity.

The previous chapter, "In defense of traits" has made a detailed case of how limiting the idea of a fixed and rigid trait is. It is not human. It is certainly not an error to be flexible and dynamic. Amidst all the evidences against the rigidity of traits, the trait theorists have managed to retain it by blaming the test items and every conceivable confounding variable for the error. But, as has been described earlier, no rational conception of item or test reliability is possible in psychological tests. Somehow, it is deemed that no change in the trait position should take place unless it permanently shifts to another position. Such changes hardly being probable in the case of the majority of the individuals, changes in the test scores were deemed to be a fault of the test itself. Unlike a thermometer where the mercury level may fluctuate from external sources of heat or movement etc. the test items do not change by themselves. Whatever be the different reactions the items elicit from the same person over different situations, it is not a shortcoming of the words or sentences. The fluctuations are not indicative of the ubiquitous error but a glimpse of the dynamic adaptation process related to various situations. Test or item scores merely reflect such changes. Whenever high reliability is apparently demonstrated, as analyzed earlier, it is an artifact of the item-analytic procedure that does not allow the tests to reflect the dynamism.

McClelland (1973) campaigned for a more dynamic approach to the measurement of ability. He wanted a test of competence in which something that grows with experience and training is conceptualized. Such a concept would reflect reality better than the abstracted and insulated IQ. In fact, these concepts allied with its unchanging nature has allowed the concept of a true score survive far beyond its utility. These concepts seem to leave human beings with a kind of pre-determinism that would do more justice to the concept of a Book of Life than to a so-called science of psychology. In the area of personality, such a case can be made even more strongly for a dynamic view of the traits and a re-conceptualization of the problem of reliability.

Validity

4.2. The formulation

Validity, as a concept, has fared little better than reliability. In fact, there has been a greater proliferation of terms contending better approximation of validity than was the case with reliability. Starting from the much-maligned Face validity, through the empirical Concurrent validity to the classic Construct validity, each, in their own way, demonstrate how impressive concepts fail miserably when it comes to translating the words into a set of acceptable steps to be followed by the test developers.

The American Psychological Association's effort to bring some semblance of order to the chaotic state of test development culminated in the Technical Recommendation for Psychological Tests and Diagnostic which started the current tripartite system of content, criterion and construct validity. The conceptualization of the three labels changed from different types of validity to different aspects or components of validity. It allowed a system to develop at the cost of stunting the challenge that these concepts should have been subjected to. In this regard, the problem of prediction of behavior has been dealt with in great detail already. Criterion validity covering the predictive validity and concurrent validity essentially refer to the same thing. The process involved in such validations is essentially that of correlating a test score with the criterion. That, in no way, provides any authenticity, a connotation attached to it by the use of the term validity. Unfortunately, validity as a concept has always implied a kind of meta-theoretical vindication of a test. On the strength of the processes involved it can only imply the extent to which the test score relates to external elements and/or the relative utility of a test and nothing beyond that.

4.2.1. Face Validity

Some supporters of face validity would say that a test must appear to measure what it is going to measure. If a test of personality used to screen army officers contains items like "Do you like ballet?" then it might look frivolous to the test-taker and might lead to non-cooperation resulting in an invalid test. This is the validity that comes in at the time of writing of the items. The Personality Research Form (Jackson, 1974) boasts more of this validity than of any other validity. However, there has been little attempt to actually measure it, though theoretically one can do so by asking some persons to key the items rather than actually respond to the contents of the test. Holden & Jackson (1979) found that items with face validity yield better results than the items having item subtlety, referring to the difficulty of relating the item to its underlying trait. The opponents of this method state that an item can very well measure a trait that was never obvious from its face validity. Statistics, rather than mere speculation (face validity seems to be little more than that) must come in to approximate the truth with empirical support. Subsequent analysis will reveal that the so-called evidence as opposed to face validity does not imply a great deal in the sense of providing a meta-theoretical reality. It is used, at least, to guide the composition of the items. Much less use has been found of the other constructs coming under the banner of validity.

4.2.2. Content validity

Content validity, in a way, would refer to how well the test samples the universe of items described by different aspects of abilities. While some consider it to be sufficient to establish the validity of a reading test (Thorndike & Hagen, 1977), others considered it to be useless (Gleser, 1969; Messick, 1975). Fitzpatrick (1983) describes in detail the sheer futility of a concept such as the content validity. She analyzed the four different aspects of content validity, such as, (1) Domain sampling, (2) Domain relevance, (3) Domain clarity, and (4) Technical quality of the items. Evaluating the state of affairs, she concluded, "These hardly approach any kind of test validity and are better understood as referring to the "content relevance", "Content representativeness", etc. of the test. The final conclusion was, "Thus no adequate meaning of content validity was found. In the light of this, it seems reasonable to conclude that content validity is not a useful term for test specialists to retain in their vocabulary" (p.11). Although this analysis was made for tests measuring abilities, it can very easily be seen to be relevant in personality research, where an universe of item content is visualized pertaining to any trait. Each test is expected to sample correctly items from that universe. Such ideas, therefore, cannot have any connotation of validity.

4.2.3. The Multitrait–Multimethod Approach

Campbell and Fiske (1959) advocated the use of multitrait-multimethod matrix (MTMM) to establish the convergent and discriminant validity of a test. Not surprisingly, it involves the use of different methods to measure the same trait as well as a few other traits. In the intercorrelation matrix obtained by correlating every test with the other, they insisted that the correlation would be the highest when both the method and trait are the same. They are the values entered in the main diagonal and reflect the reliability of the test. Next, the trait score obtained by one method would correlate highly with same trait scores obtained through other methods. These would be followed by low correlations when the traits are different but the method is same and finally the lowest correlations between tests which follow different methods as well as measure different traits. This theoretical paper also brought into focus the essential relationship between validity and reliability indices of a test.

The idea, however, lacked the mathematical rigor that would have provided the base for accepting a test as valid. But it is the logic of the approach that led Fiske, initially involved in the development of the concept, to doubt the efficacy of the method in establishing any validity (1973; 1976). However, Huba and Hamilton (1976) were not impressed and came up with a reanalysis. They used the ACL, EPPS, PRF, self-rating and peer-rating to obtain scores on Dominance, Aggression, Exhibition, Endurance, Affiliation, and Autonomy. They emphasized the essential convergence of correlations in the MMTM matrix. Fiske (1976) contended that the divergence of scores is very high when similar nature of the tests are taken into consideration. And interestingly enough, even though Murray's needs were studied, the TAT was not used in the study of Huba and Hamilton.

Fiske concluded, "any personality construct is an elusive notion that each psychologist can identify in his own perceptions and cognitions and that he can measure in his own way. An energetic researcher can apply some sample of the diverse ways of measuring a construct and pool the findings, seeking some moderately stable average picture as Huba and Hamilton have done. But what phenomena are actually depicted — behavioral responses to inventories and similar instruments?"

A researcher has the alternative of restricting himself to measurements of some sub-variety of the construct as assessed by a particular instrument and type of observer. The findings from such data will have moderate replicability and can be used in conjunction with modest theorizing about that particular perspective. Personality constructs appear to be too insubstantial to be captured by scientific operations permitting inter-subjective consensus. We seem to be near the limits for the discipline of personality based on people's construals of the behaviors they observe (Fiske, 1974). Perhaps we should try to develop a science of human interactions by analyzing the simple acts, the multiple and rapid changes in behavior, which can be identified and coded by observers who agree so nearly exactly that they are like interchangeable measuring instruments" (p. 878-879).

Fiske mildly stated that the cup was half-empty for him whereas the cup was half-full for Huba and Hamilton. But in this regard, Lumsden (1976), in his inimitable style thundered, "It is clear that the multitrait-multimethod approach should not be employed mechanically. The production of 9×9 matrices with little thought given to the selection of traits and methods should cease. It seems likely, however, that where great care has been given to test construction, where much is known *a priori* about traits, methods, and the relationship between them, the validation procedure will more and more resemble construct validation and the explicit setting up of the multitrait-multimethod matrix will be rare. It is clear that the method is not worth using badly. Is it worth the trouble of using it well?" (p. 270).

4.2.4. Construct Validity

Cronbach & Meehl's classic proper on Construct Validity (1959) had set the ideals for the test developers to follow. Before Lumsden, Fiske and Fitzpatrick and a few others did some critical analyses, validity as a concept was beyond reproach, much more than reliability ever was. Each test developer had his fond way of demonstrating validity. Construct validity was at the apex of these various ways. Giving the idea that all validities must ultimately refer to it, Cronbach *et. al.* stated, "Construct validation is involved whenever a test is interpreted as a measure of some attribute or quality which is not 'operationally defined' " (p.282). Since operationism never caught anyone's imaginations in psychometry, all measurable dimensions were accepted as constructs and were therefore felt to be in need of construct validation. Cronbach *et. al.*'s rather restrained suggestion was, "Without in the least advocating construct validity as preferable to the other three kinds (concurrent, predictive, content), we do believe it imperative that psychologists make a place for it in their methodological thinking, so that its rationale, its scientific legitimacy, and its danger may become explicit and familiar." (p.300). The way it was described, without truly giving specific answers to the problem of measuring validity, made construct validity become the all pervading stamp of real validity, an ideal to cherish.

Some psychometricians made the mistake of identifying construct validity as based on factor analysis. However impressive the mathematical sophistication might look underlying factor analysis, the inherent indeterminacy of the solutions along with the problem of factor naming etc. put the construct validity of the factors into disrepute. Factor analysis is certainly not the method to provide the unequivocal evidence of construct validity.

A critical analysis done by Lumsden and Ross (1973) of the Cronbach & Meehl's epic showed that the basic requirements of construct validation cannot be met given the present state of development of theories of individual difference. Lumsden suggested a low-keyed approach to validity based on the concept of test unidimensionality (Lumsden, 1961). But it looks usable only because it referred to items' testing ability where the aspects of unidimensionality can be specified and then similar items could be written. When it comes to personality items that ideal can hardly be reached. It will be a real hard grind to establish what are the common dimensions between just two items in a personality test. It is not clear whether a person will sit through the test that puts unidimensional questions over and over again. Asking questions like "Do you consider yourself happy-go-lucky?" then "Do you care about ups and downs in life?" and then "Does life seem enjoyable to you?" in any form will destroy any rapport established with the respondent who is likely to take it as an offence to his intelligence. Concepts like test unidimensionality and conceptual singularity always look impressive like the concept of factorially pure tests. When it comes to the numerical indexing of a beautiful ideal, everything falls well below the mark.

Lumsden concluded his critique of the unachieveability of construct validity as, "Construct validation of the tests is, therefore, impossible. It is possible that refutation of this argument, or a way out of the difficulties, will be discovered. It does seem very unlikely, however, that in any foreseeable time psychology will be able to construct and validate the equivalent of 100 or more thermometers" (p. 270). The author is in full agreement with the analysis of the constructs. But, the conclusion left the impression of some confusion about the process involved in developing a test of a construct which has been analyzed below.

4.2.4.1. Some Objections

The first implication was that instruments in sciences undergo a process called validation. The dimensions are well correlated as in the abstraction of a theory from empirical observations. The construction of a thermometer merely follows the law that heat and pressure affect the volume of liquids. The rest is a matter of choosing the suitable container and element to put it to use. If a thermometer is to be construct validated as measuring the construct of heat then the process would still have continued till now and beyond. What is heat is still being pondered over by theoretical physicists, philosophers and any one who would like to join in. They are in no better position in comprehending what makes the world go round than we are in comprehending what is intelligence. (The chapter 'In defense of traits' contains the feeling of no less a person than Einstein about it). It needs to be pointed out that the operationism of "Intelligence is what the intelligence tests measure" followed much later after the "Temperature is what the thermometers measure" explanation. This was because there were some scientists who wanted to get on with pure empirical research without being bogged down by theory. Operationism did not last long in science but that does not imply that in the so-called exact sciences the problem of construct and conceptualization is, by any means, over. Psychological constructs are multidimensional and cannot be controlled as the mercury in the thermometers can be. Moreover, the proportion of person involved in instrumentation in physics is very small in comparison with the proportion of persons trying to develop tests in psychology. An unclear thinking and lack of consensual convention has landed us in this kind of a situation where we seem to be making tremendous progress and at the same time seem to have lost direction. Another objection regarding the venture to "construct and validate" is that in psychology the two processes go together. The traditional idea of first developing a test and then thinking about the validation has been shown to be retrograde and non-tenable by Anastasi (1986). In fact, as had been suggested by Lumsden himself, validation, if at all, had to be preceded by a strong theory. That strong theory would, no doubt, color the nature of the approach taken, writing of the items, and sampling etc. which is all part of a global validation process if understood in the proper perspective.

Finally, a thermometer, because it does not show a true zero score, is found to be a convenient example of the interval scales thought to be achieved by our standardized instruments. If at all such a comparison is to be made then traits are better construed as something similar to electro-magnetic waves. These waves have at least two dimensions: the frequency and the amplitude. As has already been discussed in detail, the PI approach contends that to describe a trait more correctly a total score and any of the Dynamism Indices (from among the many possibilities mentioned) should be used.

It must be emphasized that though the analogies with physical sciences look good, such analogies have created more heart burns and confusions than have solved problems. The contention here is that our salvation lies in psychology itself. The so-called problem of validity has arisen because of our wrong conception and expectation of the construct of validity itself. It needs to be replaced with much milder utility studies that can only suggest various uses of the test. Validity of a test will not have the eye-of-God reality and authenticity.

4.3. So How Do We Develop a Test?

Before trying to answer the question it would be helpful to see the reflections of some of the leading psychometricians on this problem. While all these tremors were shaking the psychometric arena, one of the leading psychometricians, J.C. Nunnally (1978) had stated, "If a student who was uninformed about such matters asked a professor 'What are the best method for constructing tests?' the professor could answer 'it depends on many things'. In so responding, the professor would be both uninformative and incorrect, because there are straightforward, understandable, acceptable, general methods for handling 75 per cent (to guess a figure) of the needs for constructing tests." (p.256).

It should be mentioned that the same book contains an elaboration and eulogy of the true score which Lumsden must have thought he had annihilated in the year 1976. There was not even a 'with-your-leave' to Lumsden. The fact remains that few of the traditional test development processes could be adequately described as meaningful. It is not in the interest of psychometrics to go through some specified motions as conjured up by unclear thinking. In this connection Lumsden (1976) stated that he had no objection to the so-called study of reliability to be used by the students of 'transfer phenomena or fatigue etc'. Similarly, studies of validity can be used to study the semantic ability of the test-developers. There is no ground gained in carrying out the validity studies of a test. Almost as a continuation of the feeling, Anastasi (1986) bemoaned the mechanical fashion in which a test developer used to tick off the processes gone through and objective gained, as far as the tripartite aspects of content and predictive and construct validity of the test being developed were concerned. The 1985 edition of standards of educational and psychological testing has, thankfully, used a much more flexible approach. The misleading feeling it generated led to test-developers feeling relaxed after the validates of the test, such as they were, were proved. This led to the feeling of acceptance of the test scores taking on the flavor of 'eye-of-god' reality referred to before as far as true score conception was concerned.

Anastasi suggested, "The validation process begins with the formulation of detailed trait or construct definitions, derived from psychological theory, prior research, or systemic observation, and analyses of the relevant behavior domain. Test items are then prepared to fit the construct definitions. Empirical item analyses follow, with the selection of the most effective (*i.e.*, valid) item from the initial item pools. Other appropriate internal analyses may then be carried out, including factor analyses of item clusters of sub-tests. The final stage includes validation and cross-validation of various scores and interpretive combinations of scores through statistical analyses against external, real-life criteria" (p. 3). Anastasi also warned against blind empiricism. She advocated a balance between logical basis and empirical evidence for item selection. She also mentioned that the validation process is a never-ending process in which a test undergoes continuous refinements. There is no simple and straightforward answer to the question of 'How to build a valid test?' This is due, as Anastasi summarized, to the fact that "The concept of test validation has been undergoing continuing development, clarification, and refinement." (p.12). Stated with candour, even this statement has not been of much help in forcing the psychometricians to change the approach.

4.4. What Happens Then?

The obvious conclusion is that the traditional way of test development is facing obsolescence. New approaches, and new thinking has always been a painful experience for any branch which has experienced a paradigmatic stability for a period of time (Kuhn, 1970). And yet for those who want psychology to grow into a newer branch of science, an acceptance of the paradigmatic shift is essential. It will mean a violent cutting away from tradition, towards a new brand of thinking. It will involve asking different questions as well.

In this study, reliability as a concept has been replaced with the computation of individual's consistency across situations (stories) which can be used more meaningfully than the indices of test reliability. There was, therefore, no attempt to measure it, in any of the traditional sense, as reflective of the characteristics of the test. For all practical purposes, this study accepts, what Lumsden (1978) stated, "Tests are perfectly reliable."

As far as validity is concerned, the involved discussions resorted to earlier have shown that there is no validity underlying the concept of validity as used by the traditional methods. In other words, validity fails to measure what it purported to measure of the tests. The exercises reflect nothing more than just the utility of the test on a low-key basis. Lacking the bulwark of an integrated theory of personality, each test can only show if and how it is related to some demonstrated behavior indicative of the trait under consideration. This is not an ultra-operationist standpoint providing the validity but merely meeting the current need as a stop gap arrangement. The psychologists must get their act together to tackle the task of answering these questions. It is not very easy to conceptualize a suitable behavioral pattern, considering the variation in behavior accepted by the PI paradigm to establish the utility of such an approach. Beyond some theoretical possibilities, the author does not pretend to have the solutions to the questions. But the PI approach is more suited to answer the questions faced from the traditional reliability and validity perspectives.

4.5. Related Afterthought

There has been an acute proliferation of the number of tests being developed by psychologists. We psychologists cannot go on harping on the complexity of human behavior to explain such a chaotic state of affairs. If we are to study behavior then we have to accommodate what happens in real life. There are simply too many tests lying around to make an integrated approach possible. One possible way out of this would be to have a Test Development Ban Treaty (somewhat like the CTBT related to nuclear armaments) proposing a moratorium on any new type of personality tests unless supported by a theoretical standpoint. It may be pointed out that the ultimate aim of the study was not merely to replicate the EPQ but to provide the opportunity to compute various Dynamism Indices that has not been provided by any other approach, so far. If at all another trait is to be measured then it should fit into the general theory of traits, which must be suitably developed while taking its hierarchical structure into consideration. There is no way psychometrics can provide cumulative research amidst the chaos. The logic of developing 10 different tests to test any one trait, however important that might be, and each being used to validate the other without bothering about real life is thoroughly self-defeating. Statistics and mathematics are not the tools to provide the answer to problems that are essentially psychological in nature. Psychologists must sit down and thrash out a few agreements as the stepping stones to meaningful use of psychological tests, with less number of ifs and buts, towards a greater acceptance level from reality point of view.

"It's too late to correct it", said the Red Queen: "When you've once said a thing, that fixes it, and you must take the consequences."

Five

Taste of the Pudding

5. Putting the PI Idea to the Test

After reading about the amazing PI approach, which seems to be in some way contributing positively to all those diversified areas discussed earlier, one would be really looking forward to see the tests that are developed under its auspicies. This is the dreaded moment for two reasons. The first one is the possible misrepresentation of the idea of the PI approach. It should not be construed as one more of the tests. It began its career as a method of developing tests. When the idea was tested in various fields, it showed its potential, at least theoretically, in curing some of the chronic affliction of psychometrics and related areas. In that way, it is almost like a mini paradigm taking a host of interrelated view points, which might yet become a full paradigm for research in personality. However, one can still use the various tests developed under this approach without explicitly supporting the theoretical contention, just as one can use the EPQ without supporting the idea of strong genetic determinism. It needs to be emphasized that no single study, however well carried out, can establish or disprove an idea based on a logically consistent theory that is found capable of explaining the various other anomalies in related areas. While a success is a step in the right direction, a failure could be very well due to a host of factors such as one's item writing ability, sampling, and choice of the traits, etc. It might even indicate that instead of stories, short films, videos or multi-media presentation could do a better job. Disproving the PI as a viable method of testing personality has to be on grounds of limitation of its conceptualization of traits and other theoretical arguments. Traditionally, empirical evidence has been given a lot of undue importance at the cost of theory building and clear thinking. A good blend, with relatively greater importance attached to clear thinking on the problem, is attempted here.

The second reason is that with so much theoretical arguments flying around, the possibility of necessary empirical findings being underestimated could become high. And at the same time, the belief that because an idea is good it must come out crystal clear in empirical findings no matter how the data is collected could be potentially damaging. While the last chapters provide the logic and theory of the PI approach, the dust-bowl empiricism, which does not start and end with the use of statistics on any data, is clearly emphasized in this chapter. A lot of importance was given to the establishment of rapport and manner of data collection. But even before that, long arduous hours were spent in observing real life situation non-obtrusively. This provided the foundations on which the stories were based. After the skeleton was formed, care was taken to portray realism while using relatively simple expressions. Since the combinations of items and the stories were expected to provide the rationale for keying of items, items were edited to fit into a situation. Conversely, the description of the situation was also suitably modified to bring out more trait relevant expressions. When it was felt that further addition of items would be stretching the stories beyond the point of interest, which was considered very important, the first draft of the stories was accepted. The stories were repeatedly refined before the final form was accepted.

5.1. The PIAPEN

This analogue of EPQ was not named until the final stage and, in keeping with the aversion displayed towards neologisms and proliferation of jargons, the test was named PIAPEN as the acronym of Projective Inventory Analogue of Psychoticism, Extraversion and Neuroticism. The three traits are measured by the EPQ.

The PI idea has gone hand in hand with the idea of integration at the cost of proliferation and well in line with the cumulative nature of scientific endeavors. No attempt was, therefore, made to rediscover the underlying traits being studied by the PIAPEN. There was no opposition to the idea of traits and their naming as used in the traditional approaches for understanding and prediction. The opposition was merely against the rigid conceptualization of traits. The PIAPEN approach provides the flexibility whose adaptation would stretch the apparent limit of the conventional research in psychology (Fiske, 1974). So, the initial object was to be able to reproduce the trait structure of a well-known test. That being proved possible, the other additional indices could be subsequently studied in detail. This object may *prima facie* look very easy, but the theoretical analysis and the empirical evidence as reported shows that it can be very difficult to achieve. The discussion on convergent and discriminant validity has already highlighted some of the statistical problems. Psychologically also, it may well prove impossible to produce the equivalent of inventory statements with a combination of stories and relevant items as in the PI approach.

5.2. The Statements and Their Keying

There was no attempt to balance the number of trait indicative items in each story or even in the test. Writing of the items went hand in hand with the situation. In fact, some more subtleties were added into the situation allowing a larger number of items to be written. The emphasis was on avoiding any hints or suggestion of a particular act being wrong or right. In fact, the introduction to the PIAPEN specifically states this point. The introduction also suggested that the situations were gleaned from real life situation and the test-takers were to judge whether they agree or disagree with the statements that were always evaluative about the characters in the situations portrayed.

The projective hypothesis was accepted to help in the keying. There was no attempt to differentiate between projection and identification. The logic was that a person would evaluate the situation from his own perspective that could be colored by his traits. For example, in a story something happens apparently because X could not bring himself/herself to say something. When looked from an introvert's point of view, X would seem to be a person overwhelmed by the situation. An introvert, by definition, experiences the difficulty of coming out of his shell (habitual mode of responding) and would, therefore, blame the situation for his predicament. In contrast, an extrovert would not feel the difficulty and consider X to be at fault. An extravert, by definition, finds it very easy to socialize, speak out and for him possibly such a problem would not have arisen at all. So a statement regarding the situation, such as, 'X was to blame for what happened' will be responded to mostly with 'yes' by an extrovert and with 'no' by an introvert. The same logic applies to the items intended to tap the traits of neuroticism and psychoticism. While it has already been made amply clear that there is no single law of human behaviour which can cover everybody on earth, such contention as given above refers to the majority behaviour.

Here one point must be clarified. The salient aspects of experience as indicative of extraversion, neuroticism and psychoticism have already been discussed in detail. On very few occasions, any one of those aspects stands out clearly in real life situations. The only place where such aspects stand out is possibly in the inventory statements. In real life, under close scrutiny, various factors seem to contribute equally. There it is difficult to identify the only aspect in order to key the item on pure rational basis. A person behaves in a particular way because he feels that was the right thing to do at that time. He does not ask himself whether he is an extravert or an introvert and then behave accordingly. It is up to the psychologists to find out the consistencies and meanings even when there could be none.

5.2.1 A Case for Multiple Keying

Accepting the possibility that a particular behaviour might be caused by many underlying traits, multiple keying makes psychological sense. When one item can be keyed for two different traits, it is referred to as a multi-keyed item. In actual implementation of the idea, the MMPI leads the field. But most of the other inventories insist on factorial purity and single trait keying per item. Kline (1983) argues that if an item was allowed to be keyed for two traits then it would be difficult to ascertain which trait actually contributed to that item. This is surprising because psychometry left the so-called one-independent-variable experimental design and used traditional correlational design to develop the tests. This contention seems to be accepting the single causation model through the backdoor. Logically, there is nothing inviolable about the concept of single keying which could stop experimentation with multiple keying. As far as empirical tests are concerned there are a large number of scales developed from the item pool of the MMPI, which happens to be the most used inventory in the world, so far.

Moreover, factorial purity cannot be expected to be absolute given the level of sophistication achieved in measurement of traits. One has to tackle the sample variation, which makes mockery of the ideal. Helmes (1980), for example, claimed that in a Canadian sample, the EPQ did not yield the same factor structure and many items did not load in accordance with the EPQ scoring key and many items did not even load on an interpretable component. Taking nothing away from the efficacy of EPQ in the British population, this study serves to show that one cannot be too emphatic about the stability of factors. The situation becomes still unclear when issues like oblique rotation etc. are taken into consideration.

As far as PIAPEN was concerned a possible multiple keying was deemed not only acceptable but also useful from an important point of view. It would not be incorrect to describe PIAPEN as a combination of 7 tests, each test containing a situation and 30 relevant items. A total of 210 items was not very large when the objective was ultimately to generate the Dynamism Indices (DIs) over seven situations (stories) involving three traits. Increasing the total score possible in PIAPEN would entail either writing more story-statement combinations or repeating the statements relevant to a situation. None of these alternatives are very acceptable for reasons of increased testing time leading to subject boredom. If an item could function as indicative of more than one trait, then that, in effect, would add to the total score without increasing the administration time. The consequent wider variation in the scores would make a DI more discriminating. Therefore, multiple keying of items is actively sought in the PI approach.

5.2.2. The Item Format

Inventories have mostly used the two-alternative-response format where a respondent chooses between Yes/No, Agree/Disagree or True/False alternatives as a reflection of one's agreement or disagreement with the statement related to the response. Looking at the rigorous studies done about every aspect of the tests, it is a surprise that studies showing differential response to the three different types of response alternatives have not come up. On this ground, it may be taken that these pairs of responses are semantically as well as psychometrically equal. Therefore, the specific format is to be decided by the way the statements, to which they relate, were written.

The other well-known format is the forced choice one in which the respondent has to choose between two alternative statements as the most or the least descriptive of his/her characteristics. Though the EPPS utilizes this format to yield ipsative scores, one can use it to generate normative scores. In this format, the choice is between two independent items that may not be mutually exclusive. They are taken as alternatives because the two statements are scaled to be equal on social desirability scale value. In other words, both the statements are equally desirable or undesirable as descriptive of one self. But, one is forced to choose between the two, thereby, hopefully, canceling the social desirability aspect in the test.

Though the PIAPEN utilized the traditional inventory like Yes/No response, a sort of forced-choice was built-in. The juxtaposition of various opposing forces in one's day to day life was depicted clearly in the stories. So if one opposed/ supported a statement, it implied that the response was in the face of the existence of the opposing inclinations described in the story. To that extent, the PI approach attempted an integration of the two formats.

Velicer and Stevenson (1978) contended that a seven-choice response format seemed more promising on the ground of, (1) Allowing the subject to make finer distinction, (2) Increased item and scale reliability, (3) Favourable subject's reaction, and (4) A clear and more accurate indication of factor structure. In their study, the Eysenck's Personality Inventory showed an improvement in the clarity of factor structure when the seven-choice item format was used. While not denying its use for further research and analysis in the PI approach, it must be clarified that the PIAPEN had a limited objective to achieve. It had nothing to do with the rediscovery of the factor structure in the personality arena. The aim was merely to develop through the PI approach a set of items that would function as test of the PEN factors as measured by the EPQ. It was decided that a two alternative Yes/No type response format will help in achieving that objective. With the hindsight of the difficulties involved in actually computing the DIs, it can be safely stated a wider variation of scores in each item would be more helpful than the two response items.

The First Attempt

5.3. The Rationale and the Objective

The first attempt was to develop a British version of the PIAPEN. Its high pedigree may not be obvious but can easily be inferred from the steps taken to develop it. Just sort of asking Prof. Eysenck himself to write the stories and items, all possible steps were taken to ensure that the traits were tapped. A thorough reading of the EPQ items and the manual as well as other related documents was undertaken to appreciate Eysenck's points of view. It is not a very easy thing to do when one does not share the basis of the viewpoint. Be that as it may, with Eysenck's perspective taken, independent keying of items by the author coincided with the EPQ's original keying. First a possible combination of situation and statements were thought of. Then some real life observations were also made. Those combined with a year-old appreciation of British life (as distinct from Indian) provided the skeleton. The statements were then filled in. There was inter-dependence between the story structure and the items. Sometimes items were deleted to trim some part of the story which seemed far fetched and sometimes the story was expanded to fit in the items. After the author's supervisor did the all-important job of smoothing the obvious jagged ends and refining of expressions etc., the PIAPEN was ready to be put to test.

In this study, the EPQ was chosen as the model after which the first attempt at a PI analog would develop. Though there was no need to have a rationale for this choice, EPQ was found suitable for many reasons. The robustness of the model and the replicability of the factors of Psychoticism, Extraversion and Neuroticism had been well recorded and also the reasons analyzed in the previous chapter. Over and above that, the EPQ had established itself firmly in the international sphere and widely used in India either in a translated version or in its original form. Moreover, it provided a compact test with only three traits scores and one Lie score but which fits into a system. That was thought to be a better proposition than what would have been possible with some other choice of traits from other tests. The factors were distinct (orthogonal) and it was thought to be an easier task to write stories and items for those traits having such a base. And finally, English being the common language that separates U.K. from U.S.A., why not use a test (a British one) that the British would understand? Though we Indians are still struggling with this concept, in Britain, it seemed like a great idea and it was duly followed.

There were five stories portraying various situations in British life. It must be accepted that the author's limited experience of the British culture proved to be one of the many stumbling blocks. It was the beginning of the research project that ostensibly aimed at developing a test on PI lines to counter social desirability. From that point of view it was deemed necessary to have a pilot study to get the feel of the British testing situation and the responses it yielded.

5.3.1 A Pilot Study

It must be mentioned that it was the period of sticking to the tradition and following the lines of great sayings. The idea was to administer the test on its own to find out the internally consistent items providing four different scores (P, E, N and L) as was strongly advocated by Nunnally (1978) and supported by Kline (1983). In fact, Kline reported that he had to resort to this process as he found difficulty in the clear emergence of factors in his own study. Therefore, this process of item analyses was followed. The subsequent plan, granting the possibility of a sizable number of items left after the analysis, was to administer the test along with EPQ on another sample to find out the correlation and the agreement of the PIAPEN scores providing the authenticity to the theoretical contention. In the third stage, it was hoped that an explicit study to test the SD resistance of the PIAPEN as opposed to the EPQ could be conducted providing the grand finale to the efforts.

5.3.2. The Sample and Testing

Usually, it is after the data was collected and analyzed, disproving some of the researcher's undue optimism, that one feels the pang of pessimism. But for the author, it came quite easily and in the form of utter despair. Unlike the willing student population in India (Orissa to be specific) British student population strongly believed that they were extremely busy. An initial effort to ease the problem of individual administration was made by the author being introduced to a class. The test booklets were handed over to the students and they were requested to return the booklets as early as possible. That yielded about 30 responses, returned after varying period of time. After that, personal approach on an individual basis requesting their help in research was resorted to. It must be emphasized that there was a feeling of resentment about the fact of being tested (by the author?) which was reflected in the difficulty in getting back the questionnaires. Allowing the respondents longer period of time and requesting them to complete it at their own leisure did not help the matter. It must be emphasized that there were neither course credits nor any financial incentive to offer to put only a temporary stop to the extreme business of the students. In desperation, the help of other persons with wide variation in background was taken. Still, the progress was slow and tortuous. The outlook of being able to complete the other stages of the research seemed very bleak. After about six months and an assorted bunch of 100 test responses, the idea of a British PIAPEN was rather unceremoniously shelved. This episode was seen as a limitation of the author and not of the idea of the PI being suitable for the British climate.

5.3.3. Data Analysis

The data was not analyzed statistically. But the data collection process yielded qualitative information that was found to be very useful. There were valuable insights gained and lessons learnt through this episode. There were some useful comments, mostly verbal and a few recorded ones. Informal analysis of the test was done to find out if there was a lack of clarity that possibly led to the high subject attrition. The author himself, his supervisor and another post-doctoral researcher keyed the items for the traits of the test. It was found that they could agree on 27 out of 104 items. It must be mentioned that the items and the stories looked to be all right before the pilot study. It is only after the failure that a rethink was called for. Though the number commonly agreed upon stood for better-than-chance judgement, it was certainly not very encouraging from the point of view of the development of the test. The complexity of sentences used in the statements was thought to be the cause of the low agreement. Interestingly, this itself was taken as the evidence for projective processes underlying our judgment.

Some test-takers had complained that the test was too long and that it took them more than three hours, while others had reported that they could do it in an hour. Some called it melodramatic whereas others rated it 4 on a 5-point realism scale (5 being true to reality). There were attempts to analyze the nature of the test. Some conjectured that it was a test of difference between rich and poor etc. Some of these observations were codified. This provided the author with some evidence of something akin to projection taking place in the testing situation. After this valiant attempt, the author felt discretion to be better part of valor and decided to go back to India for a fresh attempt to develop PIAPEN suitable for the Indian climate.

The Second Attempt

5.4. The Rationale and the Objective

The past failure paved the way for a better understanding of the processes. With a view to give the test the fairest of chances, stories were written, adopting those five stories into Indian context and adding two more. For item analytic purpose, the number of items in each story was increased to 30 items. In Orissa, the author's native state in India, students learn English at a very early stage in the schools. But, for the sake of avoiding ambiguities, the English used in the test was deliberately kept at a very simple level. The statements used were straightforward. The main characters in the stories were mostly students who were the target for the development of the test. Another significant difference was that no obvious attempt was made to key the item for L score. The argument was that if at all PIAPEN was resistant to the SD effect, such L score items provided useless information while increasing the administration time. The draft stories and items underwent refinements till they were ready to be put to test. Puhan himself expressed the feeling that if at all the PI idea was to catch the imagination then the PIAPEN had to be the best bet. As already mentioned in the introductory chapter the study was undertaken more with a purpose of exploding a myth than to eulogize one's own brand of panacea.

It cannot be emphatically stated that the idea of such an outcome proving more likely by utilizing a test of such pedigree did not cross the author's mind.

5.4.1. The Sample

After the initial set back in the tentative pilot study in Britain, it was deemed necessary to pinpoint the sample and the objective of the test. The study aimed to develop the PIAPEN in order that it would be used to study the senior undergraduate and postgraduate students in Orissa, a state in India. 242 male and 237 female students from undergraduate colleges and postgraduate departments under Utkal University participated in the testing sessions.

5.4.2. Testing

Wherever possible, the administrations of tests were made in small groups of 10-15 students in a session. The teachers who took their classes introduced the author to the students. After the introduction, participants were told that the experiment was aiming to develop the test. It was emphasized and clarified that no individual in particular was being tested. They were categorically asked not to write their name, age, and sex, which would in someway identify them. They were told that the author was merely interested in the average response of the student population. The participants were encouraged to feel free and give their frank responses. In Orissa, the students need a lot of encouragement and reassurance really to feel free. And it was hard work trying to achieve that.

Everybody was encouraged to ask questions and freely express their feelings. It was done to ensure that the respondents did not feel to be under any constraints to complete the test. They were also encouraged to write their comments at the end if they so liked The author expected some resentment from the students on the restriction of response that a Yes/No response format usually entails. As reported earlier, the EPPS with its forced choice format yielded resentment in some cases and the author was interested in finding such cases in the PIAPEN that had forced-choice characteristic built-in. But no verbal or written complaints or comments were reported.

It must be mentioned that there was a fair bit of good humor flying about in the testing session. The serious attitude to test taking which mostly ends up putting the test-takers on the defensive was avoided. To reassure the test-takers, they were encouraged to ask questions about any aspect, including the author, in the testing situation. There were not many forthcoming in the test situation itself. But after the session, quite a few queries regarding life and research in Britain were made. They expressed their incomprehension of the fact that the author having gone from India to Britain for research had to come back to India for research and again would have to go back to Britain for further research and then to come back to India for continuing research. Though the author could not provide an adequate answer, those queries provided good evidence of general rapport that was established.

No time limit was stipulated to complete the tests. The test-takers were never pressed to go through the tests quickly, but they could finish both the EPQ and the PIAPEN well within two hours. For the record, the tests were administered in such a way that half of the times EPQ was followed by PIAPEN and rest of the times it was *vice versa*. The answer sheets were collected in pairs so that the two tests belonging to an individual could be identified. Two piles were made apparently for convenience but the responses of male and female students were in different stacks for the analysis of any systematic difference.

There was a particularly interesting experience, during the data collection, which sheds light on our concept of unambiguous sentences. There was a student who seemed to have got stuck on an item of EPQ. After checking with the watch that 10 minutes had elapsed on that one item, the author decided to intervene and asked if he could help the respondent. The item was, "Do you have many different hobbies?" What was worrying the respondent was the use of the expression 'many different'. He could not respond because he was not sure what the expression meant because he did have many hobbies but was not sure whether they were many different hobbies., Frankly, the author himself did not know what to say and simply asked the respondent to go on to the other items and come back to that later. This showed how ambiguity lies in our heads and just by instructing the subjects not to think too much about it would not take it away.

5.4.3. Data Analysis

In the introduction, attempts have been made to shed new light on old problems and, in the process, old data and some personal data have been analyzed. Those, conventionally, should have featured in this part of the thesis but has actually come up in the introductory part. Those analyses are integral parts of the contention and should be taken as the beginning of the analytic process. Here, whatever sense could be made through various statistical processing of the data collected by administering PIAPEN and EPQ together on 479 students will be discussed.

5.4.3.1. Scoring

In the interest of objectivity, it was decided to use empirical keying to choose the items for selection. Therefore, the 210 PIAPEN items were arbitrarily keyed '1' for 'yes' response and '0' for 'no' response in each case. The item, which had no response, was recorded as missing. There was no intention of rediscovering the true factor structure of the EPQ. The intention was to locate those items that would load on the factors indicated by the total score on the three scales. Therefore, the total scores of Extraversion, Neuroticism and Psychoticism were computed to serve as the markers for the final factor identification and item selection.

5.4.3.2. On Using Factor Analysis

One feels privileged if s/he can use a sophisticated data analytic measure rather than a simple one. It is not so when one uses factor analysis. Stepping into factor analysis means stepping into troubled waters. Harman's Factor Analysis (1976) is deemed to be one of the authoritative books on the topic. It is referred to for many authoritative pronouncements regarding how to get the data factor-analyzed. The author would, however, like to quote Harman, who in the introductory note cited the following quotation of Cureton (1939, p. 287):

"Factor theory may be defined as a mathematical rationalization. A factor-analyst is an individual with a peculiar obsession regarding the nature of mental ability or personality. By the application of higher mathematics to wishful thinking, he always proves that his original fixed idea or compulsion was right or necessary. In the process he usually proves that all other factor-analysis are dangerously *insane*, and that the only salvation for them is to undergo his own brand of analysis in order that the true essence of their several maladies may be discovered. Since they never submit to this indignity, he classes them all as hopeless cases, searches about for some branch of mathematics which none of them is likely to have studied in order to prove that their incurability is not only necessary but also sufficient" (p.10)

Although Harman mentioned that the heated controversy about which is the best method of factor analysis was over, it can be shown to be wrong. Some researches (*e.g.*, Hashemi, 1981; Cooper, 1982) still defend their discovered combination as the only way to salvation. The author has scrupulously stepped away from making any such statements. There is strong logic behind it, besides the quotation from Cureton. Ultimately, the taste of the pudding must lie in the eating. No mathematics, however efficient it is deemed to be (it has to be only a little better in comparison with the alternatives) can override the psychological consideration. Ultimately, tests developed with the help of item factor analytic procedure have to undergo much more referring and cross checking before their uses are brought to the acceptable level. When huge sample fluctuations in the correlations reported even in case of established inventories (which, of course, one can shrug off as one of those things) such arguments are pointless. To the uninitiated, computers have been providing help of rather dubious kind in such matters. On one hand, computers permit one to factor analyze data without needing to know anything *via* the God-send (to the petrified souls) *default options*. On the other hand, they provide the option of running multitudes of factor extraction programs. The hapless being's perplexity is increased multifold when that is combined with the choice of various method of deciding on the number of factors to be extracted. That perplexity is, undoubtedly, multiplied by the number of options for rotation offered, not to forget the option of 'no rotation' as well. It might look frivolous if it is suggested that even computers grumble. Those who have been rather over-enthusiastic about testing and had too many items (like the author, for example) may discover run-time checks, error messages (which appear to be meant for the eyes of some NATO generals rather than the lesser mortals like research students) etc. very similar to computer discontentment.

5.4.3.3. The Preliminary Analysis

The statistical package SPSSX was used for the analyses. A preliminary analysis was carried out using the default options which was Principal Components Analysis (PCA) with Varimax rotation. Varimax rotation was accepted because the EPQ is supposed to be a robust test consisting of 3 orthogonal factors. The default criteria for retaining factors for rotation was that the Eigen values be greater than unity. Male and Female data for the preliminary analysis were treated separately. The results were unexpected. With so much care taken to write the statements and the type of sample chosen it was expected than the items load on 3 factors mostly. But, the male data yielded 80 factors while the female data yielded 82 factors. A recent study of the factorial structure of MMPI revealed that about 144 factors could be extracted from 550 items (Johnson *et al.*, 1984). To the less optimistic it might have looked disastrous, but with the author blessed with rather quixotic optimism it seemed like PIAPEN following in the footsteps of the famous MMPI. However, Johnson *et al.* ultimately settled down to about a score of factors. The PIAPEN data could similarly been analyzed to reduce the number of factors to a reasonable level. But in this case, given the situation and the different perception that each statement can produce, the author could not have progressed very far even with ten factors. In fact, such an exercise was hardly of any use from the point of view of the objective of this study. The only obvious conclusion was that the idea of PI was a non-starter or something was grossly wrong with the way the traits were conceptualized by the author and measured by the PIAPEN. With the elaborate steps taken and cross checked by Puhan that seemed to be not so correct a decision even in the face of such data. So, ultimately the author turned to psychology to provide the answer.

5.4.3.4. A Looking Back

It was formulated, in the course of the discussion on the trait concept, that tests developed under the PI approach would encourage variation in human behavior that could be not only idiosyncratic but also possibly a function of the situation. The stories were written keeping that in mind. In contrast, the conventional approach (like the EPQ approach) strives to eliminate variation. The nature of the items ensures that a clear factorial structure will emerge. In contrast, from the PI perspective, the fact of getting the unwieldy factor structure using the total sample is not really that unexpected. It had been previously analyzed that in real life situations most of the people, lying in the mid-range of the distribution, will not maintain their rank order position. In the PIAPEN, it would imply a highly attenuated correlation at the inter-item level as well as with the marker scores. There is no way that the EPQ scores could be changed to reflect the flexibility of the PIAPEN. But the PIAPEN could be adopted to meet the rigid criteria of the EPQ. As has been discussed earlier, at the extreme end of the range of scores, the variability of the individual decreases and could become more consistent as the traits like the PEN are conceptualized. To meet the objective of developing the EPQ equivalent, the correct approach would be, therefore, to reduce the noise in the mid-range and then to analyze the intercorrelation.. Such an approach will not yield a correlation if there is no correlation in the total sample, *i.e.*, if the distribution of sample scores is circular. But if the distribution is elliptical, the correlation will be more distinctive, reflective of the correlation that would have emerged had homoscedasticity been present.

This argument, when found defensible, was utilized for data reduction for the purpose of computation of correlation. As a starter, scores falling in mid range from Mean – 1SD to Mean + 1SD were chosen for elimination. It was hoped that successive increase in the limits of the range for eliminate would possibly lead to the objective if the first attempt failed. This range was chosen because while it reduced scores by 68%, it still left enough scores to take care of any random fluctuations like subject disinterest, encoding error etc. Moreover, the pair-wise deletion option leaves essentially the same number of scores for computation of correlation while providing opportunity of maximizing the correlation with each of the markers.

Some changes in the factor analytic procedure were also deemed necessary after the initial optimism was lost. It was decided that after maximizing the correlation with the markers the initial factor extraction would be sufficient to indicate which of the items load on which factor to facilitate factor naming. Only 3 factors were to be extracted to see if the markers load individually in those factors. There was really no ground to think that there should be any difference between the male and female data. Moreover female and male respondents number only 237 and 242 respectively. The number fell sadly below Nunnally's level of 10 respondents per variable but reassuringly near Kline's stipulation of 2 respondents per variable. It is a bit difficult to appreciate the mathematical proof that permits such a wide variation as a specification. In any case, the 1:2 ratio seemed like something closer to the survival routine. The ratio not being maintainable for separate analysis of the male and female data, it was deemed only necessary to look at the factor structure of male and female data. If no obvious differences were seen, the data would be merged for final analysis that would determine item selection.

5.4.3.5. *Final Analysis*

The results were as surprising in the positive sense as they were in the negative sense when more than 80 factors in both the cases were extracted. Table 1 demonstrates the comparative factor loading of the markers in the male and female data.

TABLE 1

Loading of the Markers in Male and Female Data

Markers	M/F	Factor 1	Factor 2	Factor 3
N Score	M	.41835	-	-
	F	.41546	-	-
P Score	M	-	.30224	-
	F	-	.31136	-
E Score	M	-	-	-
	F	-	-	-

(The criterion for suppression was <.20 loading.)

The factorial matrices were very close to the one that was hypothesized in both the cases. There was quite a lot of similarity in the items, which loaded into the three factors. In both the cases, the three factors explained 12.7 percent of the variance. The markers N and P loaded substantially and singly in the first two factors. However, the third factor was less encouraging. The marker E loaded comparatively higher in the third factor but fell below the suppression criterion of .20 loading by a small margin in both male and female samples. There were low correlations among the 3 factors.

The main purpose was to see that the factor solutions were, more or less, the same. From that point of view, the result was quite encouraging for the next analysis. The data was then merged and analyzed.

The factor matrix of the combined data was even more

encouraging. While markers P and N loaded .53515 and .43094 in the first and second factors respectively, the marker E loaded .30283 in the third factor. Factor identification was obvious and clear-cut. More importantly, most of the items loading on to different factors significantly made psychological sense providing a proof of the efficacy of the using the total PEN scores as markers in the study. While a few of items did load highly on more than one factor, most of the items selected clearly load on single factors. A rather stringent criterion for selection would unduly restrict the number of items and, consequently, also restrict the range of the proposed Dynamism Index. Moreover, it has already been argued about why it is worthwhile to allow multiple keying. Therefore, for the final item selection, a loading of .30 was stipulated as the minimum criterion. That yielded a total of 54 items for psychoticism, 46 items for neuroticism and 32 items for extraversion scales. Items were keyed for traits if they loaded more than .30 on one or more of the factors.

It was deemed possible that some of the stories may prove less cost-effective in the sense that they yield a rather a small number of trait items in comparison with other stories. As can easily be seen such clear-cut distinction was not demonstrated in the item analyses. It meant that there will be no substantial reduction in the administration time, given the importance attached to the comprehension of the situation (stories). But indirectly, it proved quite encouraging to the author whose own projection into the situation was commented upon by Puhan in the writing stage. It is also heartening from a normative point of view that idiographic experiences can be used for normative studies because empathy, projection and identification are shown to be more general processes that make the idiosyncratic perception of individual more or less comparable. Since there is no difference between the stories of the initial version and the final one Appendix C contains only the selected items in the different stories for the final version of the PIAPEN. Appendix D provides the keying of the items. The multiple keyed items are easily located and can be ignored if one feels inclined to do so. Such items show the flexibility of the approach but do not form a necessary part of the approach.

"Would you tell me, please, which way I ought to go from here?"
"That depends a good deal on Where you want to go to", said the cat.

Six

Towards a Better Future

6. At the End of the Day

Everything must come to an end and one must prepare for the reception. Of course, before that, one needs to have a good look at the object of the reception. It is one thing to argue about various theoretical points. It is another thing to translate the theories into a set of items that will do what the theories indicated it would do. This is not to deny the role played by theory. On the contrary, building up a theoretical basis is deemed essential for the best possible use of statistics for analyses and ultimate use of empirical findings.

In the earlier chapters, the theoretical basis of the PI approach was built. It needs to be bolstered further by a theory of personality which can accomodate hierarchical trait structures. At the lower end of the spectrum one can expect the PI approach to function as a highly viable method of developing tests, and at the higher end it will be a mini paradigm on which a whole range of social psychological, mathematical and differential psychological research can be conducted to shed light on this complex area. It will help in understanding and predicting behaviour. All these possibilities can be realized only if the tests managed to retain sufficient items in at least a majority of the stories, permitting the computation of the various indices of dynamism. Such computations have been discussed in great detail in the chapter on the dynamic conception of trait. Here only a short description is given to bring home to users the possibilities.

A test, under the PI approach, consists of combinations, each characterized by a description of a situation (stories) followed by some statements regarding the situation. If, for example, at least 5 items for each of the traits are retained in the stories then it can be possible to have a score variation from 0 to 5. This could be used to compute the group mean and standard deviation for each of the stories. One way of computing a DI of a person is to compute the Z scores of his performance in each of the stories, separately. A total of the Z scores would provide an index of the personal deviation with regard to the group's mean across situations. Another DI regarding a person's personal deviation over situation can easily be computed by computing the variance of the Z scores as scored by the individual across relevant stories. Over and above these, stories can be scaled for demand characteristics and each person's performance can be seen against the backdrop of the situational forces. The use of the different indices, therefore, depends on the research or application need of the user. It is not essential that all such indices be computed of the individual. It should be determined by the level of understanding of human behaviour at that stage. If the item analysis reveals that there are enough number of items left in the related stories then it would be considered a success. In view of the active promotion of variation in the test, it was very surprising that a large number of items were selected. They were also uniformly distributed over all the stories. From a purely empirical point of view, all the stories provide very good opportunity to compute the dynamism indices relating to each of the three factors. But, mere computation hardly furthers one's knowledge. It is essential that a proper analysis of what these indices stand for and what group to look for a comparison as regards the utility of the dynamism indices be theoretically analyzed and empirical steps thought of. In this research it was realized that some aspects of the study be subjected to more thinking and theoretical explanations to make full use of the empirical indices.

On the other side Puhan and his associates have produced quite a few tests under the PI approach analogous to different scales of the California Psychological Inventory (Banu, 1981; Puhan and Roy, 1985 ; Puhan and Dash, 1985; Patnaik, 1985). Approaching the problem of test development in traditional ways, Puhan found the tests showing high convergent validity while the discriminant validity was low. Some research into the effects of SD as initially contended has been adequately studied. But in view of the previous analysis regarding the social desirability effects, the studies have limited implication as the PI approach was studied in this piece of research. Puhan's approach is to develop a large number of scales through the PI method in order to establish a foot hold in the testing arena, a presence of the method which cannot just be wished or smiled away for the lack of numbers. In the uncertain world of traditional psychometrics, where piling up of evidences of reliabilities and validities of even the so-called established tests is resorted to, the idea that quantity will ultimately produce quality can be seen as a sound policy for cumulative research and survival. This, however, has never been the approach as proposed in this book.

One would feel a bit perplexed by the way the factor of Psychoticism has cropped up so saliently as the first factor extracted in the analysis. As reported by Kline and Barrett (1983), Extraversion tends to be much more robust a factor than Psychoticism, a late entrant into competition for existence in the trait arena. Moreover, the theorization of an Extraversion factor has been more easily accepted than that of Psychoticism factor. But an analysis of the item-situation combination in the PIAPEN indicates a rather strong tendency on their parts to reflect aggression or unconventionality more than they do reflect the other aspects. This is possibly because the reported elusiveness of psychoticism provided a subtle bias to tap that trait more. This analysis is done with wisdom of hindsight. As far as possible, the stories were written to make the situation comprehensible, short and yet, vivid. The items were written which could justifiably be traced back to have the origin in the situation, even when one can ask some of the questions without referring to the situation at all. A more realistic picture was deemed more essential than an obvious tapping of traits. In other words, the author being doubtful about the process of projection, greater care was provided to facilitate the process, if any, than about the statement part of the test. This was hoped to be achieved by dropping items having any obvious or suggested responses.

The other possible explanation is that in India, society still has a larger say over individual freedom, a factor of unconventionality or aggressiveness may become more salient than the factor of extraversion. It cannot be overemphasized that in India, socialization tends more towards the internalization and less towards verbalization of regards, love, and appreciation, etc. Whether a child is extraverted or introverted is deemed less important and is less discernible. The comparable scores may be higher cross-culturally implying that Indians (including the Oriyas) are less extraverted than the British. The extraction of factors in the order of Psychoticism, Neuroticism and Extraversion may very well point towards the relative importance ascribed to the traits in the Oriya society, at least for the group of respondents who took part in experiment. On the other hand, it may all be an artifact of the testing situation. In other words, it could be the end product of individual's perception of the story and statement combination. While the latter possibility remains, the fact that a few surprises can be logically explained referring to real life situation definitely adds to the strength of the case.

One can criticize the criteria of .30 loading on the factor containing the marker score as too lax for the purpose of factor identification. Helps (1981) had pointed out that no less an authority than Eysenck did the same! One can easily refer to the tables and see that using a higher criterion for item selection would end up in yielding less number of items that would be closure to the EPQ structure of PEN factors both in number and may even be in robustness. Only if the intention was merely to produce a parallel form of the EPQ then such a step could be defended. But the major interest in this approach was to produce the Dynamism Indices indicative of deviation of a person's score over the situations. In order to be able to do that there should be a sizable score possible in each of the situations. That would require more items to be selected in each of the selected stories. A criterion of .30 loading has yielded just about the right number of items. This is evident from the highest score possible in each trait. Psychoticism items yield highest scores of 8, 8, 5, 6, 4, 6 and 12, respectively over stories from A to G. When multi-keyed items are added (5 more items) such scores increase to 9, 8, 5, 8, 6, 6 and 12. Neuroticism items yield scores of 4, 5, 7, 6, 7, 4 and 7, which become 5, 6, 8, 6, 8, 4 and 9 with the addition of 6 multi-keyed items across the stories. Extraversion yields scores of 3, 6, 5, 2, 4, 3 and 3, which added with 6 multiple keyed items become 5, 7, 5, 3, 4, 3, 5 across situations. As is evident, the multi-keyed items would help in the increase of scores without unduly increasing the total number of items that would help in sustaining subject's interest and cooperation.

The initial objective thus achieved, the author feels a five point scale would not only be useful on the grounds of greater satisfaction of the respondent but also, equally importantly, would yield a larger score variation without increasing the number of items in the test. It might prove to be more acceptable than the use of multi-keyed items for increasing score variability. This should be studied in greater detail for incorporation into the PI approach as an integral part.

6.1 About Item Selection and Keying

Even though the author strongly feels about the primacy of human logic over statistics, the empirical findings have to be given their recognition. The reason is not a sudden loss of faith in that process but an acceptance of the essential indeterminacy of the trait salience (evidence of multiple causation?) in different situations. As a matter of curiosity as well as of research interest, Kline keyed the items as did two other postgraduate students. If the items were thought to be much more straightforward than the items of the unsuccessful attempt, one could expect a sizable agreement. What was more noticeable was their disagreement. The postgraduate students were friends of the author. They were assured that any comment, however harsh or seemingly far-fetched, would be welcome. That included the possibility of refusing to key the items on grounds of incomprehension of Indian culture and the portrayed situations. While other observations regarding the Indian English (a world standard English spoken by vast population) were made, nobody reported incomprehension of the situation (three cheers for the normative approach!). The author deliberately stayed out to maintain objectivity. The keying revealed a difference in the trait conceptualization itself when it referred to some specific situation. Under such circumstances, it was deemed better to leave the judgement to the respondents. In other words, purely empirical keying was opted for. However, the agreement between Kline's keying and the empirical keying was really surprising. Of course, Kline did have some experience and insight into the Indian culture. Still, the agreement in the keying was very impressive. While it did not wash away the author's skepticism in one swift clear stroke, it definitely provided for a welcome change. It kindled more than just a flicker of hope. Be that as it may, for the time being, a completely empirical keying has been adhered to with the hope that further research will clarify the issue of keying.

The multiple keying idea as could be used by the PI approach was first mooted here. It was possible because only in this attempt of test development under the PI approach there has been attempts to study more than one trait in each story. The idea can be explored further as the logicality of multiple keying has been hinted at earlier. And yet, to maintain defensibility both the types of item keying (single and multiple) are clearly identified in the relevant table. Instead of forcing a decision, which does not have a strong base, the decision of item keying is left to the user.

While trying to analyze the social desirability effect and

the various attempts to tackle the problems, the sheer futility of such exercises gradually became evident. From that point, it was a very hard task trying to convince oneself as well as others by analyzing the data given as evidence and the recommendations by leading psychometricians that the so-called problem of social desirability is not a problem at all but a misunderstanding of the processes involved. Far from invalidating the tests by its presence, it merely shows that all the traits have social learning connotation. The analysis has provided the necessary bridge for the gap between social and differential psychology. Having come to such a conclusion, it was hard to find any meaning in the exercise of trying to develop another method of testing the same traits for which tests already exist. In other words, the conclusion took away the very rationale of the study as conceived in the beginning. And yet, the analysis provided a valuable insight into the theory of opposing forces in every trait dimension which also helped in understanding some of the problems involved in related areas.

That led this study into the so-called situation verses trait controversy. The conceptualization of rigid traits always made the author very uncomfortable because it was less reflective of reality, when compared to the variations and inconsistencies found in the social life. To cap it all, Prof Kline's faith in the trait of Extraversion and the author's complete lack of it provided the main interest in trying to find some use of the test. It must be emphasized here that the idea of PI approach as containing different stories to depict various situations was not just fortuitous. It was modeled after Hartshorne and May's situational tests with a high cost-benefit advantage over it, provided that the PI approach actually worked. It was thought that characteristics of the test could help in providing some kind of solution to the controversy.

Instead of trying to eradicate the wrongly conceived SD effect, the PI approach was found capable of generating many more indices of human dynamism than has been offered by any test. Combined with the dynamic conceptualization of traits, such indices were theorized to be helpful in providing the answer to low correlation with the criterion in the predictive use. This approach supports idiothetic as well as idiographic research by providing intraindividual dynamism indices. Nomothetic approach, possibly would gain the most because the whole idea of consistency is seen from a different perspective. No point is gained in arguing about why in behavioural measures, in spite of the rigidity of traits, individuals show inconsistency. Instead, a dynamic conception of trait expects the manifestations of some behavioural inconsistency which is accepted as normal giving due respect to the individuality of the individual. The PI approach helps in the computation of indices of such variation and enables the user to decide on how much inconsistency he requires or finds acceptable. As has been analyzed in detail, such an approach tries to integrate the different findings in the related area.

All these possibilities were not very easily conceived. But, after seeing the potentiality, a strong theoretical case was made out. Of course, it must be accepted that visualizing the possible uses and actually devising experiments to test those are different ball games. Further research is needed to provide the empirical evidence. In the PIAPEN, though it is deemed easy to compute the dynamism indices as has been conceptualized in the chapter on traits, the actual computation was not attempted as it would not provide any extra information than the idea behind them provide. In fact, such computation will capitalize on the chance factor that occurs when the initial and crosscheck samples are the same. As has been suggested, a number of studies are needed to carry out investigation into the various uses of each of those indices. The numbers of items left in the stories for each of the traits of Psychoticism, Neuroticism, and Extraversion are encouragingly similar and relatively large. That would theoretically make variations in the trait score of the individuals possible. But the outcome of the analysis has exceeded the most optimistic expectation of the author. Carrying out further research using the PIAPEN will not be hampered by the lack of variation in the stories. In case it was found that in spite of the number of items in a story it fails to produce the required or meaningful variation, then such stories will not be used for computing the variation of that particular trait. As is now very obvious, the PIAPEN provides one of the most flexible and realistic alternatives to the traditional approaches. Even for those who feel very insecure while treading on new trails can find solace in the fact that a higher selection criteria, and summing up of trait scores across situations will bring back that feeling of being at home with the familiar EPQ.

To be consistent with the PI approach with its attempt to sample variation, the idea of a test reliability was not found to be very helpful. Merely theorizing that the test reliability was actually individual reliability was not expected to solve the problem. That led to the venture of analyzing the whole gamut of psychometric processes deemed as essential for the development of a test in the traditional sense. Very interestingly, the same concepts, which were once accepted without opposition, were found crumbling under attack from various sources. It was pathetic to see when every aspect of psychology is wrought with controversy, this area has stayed insulated from such upheavals patronized by unclear thinking and slavish acceptance of the supremacy of number over anything logical and psychological. In any case, test reliability with the whole host of indices were thoroughly ignored in this research not because of the test's or author's inability to do so, but because the theoretical analysis revealed them to be exercises in futility. As far as validity is concerned it was found lacking in the mythical power of vindicating the efficacy of tests either empirically or traditionally. The only thing that was inferred to be usable is that validity indices are simply utility measures reflecting merely the correlation of the test with the criterion. Trying to achieve an agreement to cut down on the number of tests lying around (weapons control) to allow the psychometricians to think about some solution (the author did not have any) to the problem was also analyzed. With the high loadings of the items on the three factors, a high index of validity (convergent, criterion or whatever) could be peddled. This was not done to be consistent with the standpoint of starting a new thinking on the processes of testing. Such ventures are much more difficult than piling up validity and reliability indices.

These provided the theoretical support whose development had been the dominating feature of this research. The theory of dynamic traits combined with the PI approach had been able to find relevance in the various contributing areas of research. Of course, mere theory has hardly any chance of survival without the so-called solid empirical evidence. The evidence provided by the higher number of items loading on different factors and the selection of all the seven stories strongly vindicated the new conceptualisation of traits and the PI approach to testing personality. It did not merely show that an analog with all the frills is possible but it also provided a scope for computing and using the Dynamism Indices in future research. The fact of the existence of such a test will encourage a new kind of research planning and thinking which was not possible with the inventories yielding a single score for each trait. Admittedly all such indices could be computed by analyzing the response to the various pictures used in projective tests. The difficulty obviously will be in generating enough of score variation in each of the pictures to make the computation of the Dynamism Indices meaningful. That is the highlight of the empirical achievement of this research.

The progress of this research has turned out to be an elaborate Mark Anthony's speech. The only difference was that in the beginning there was much stronger interest to bury Caesar than to praise him. But it is no shame to accept the potential when reason and evidence show how much of that is present. Of course, in the western world, blowing one's own trumpet (if you don't, then who will?) is deemed to be an integral part of self-sufficiency and rugged individualism and should not cause undue dismay. For all practical purposes the results of the study has exceeded the expectation. That reminds one of Rasch's (1960) discomfiture when his model provided a near perfect fit to the criterion behaviour. Granting the fact that the an unconventional approach has been adopted, improvizations had been resorted to (which one may comment as rather opportunistic), the agreement between the theory and empirical evidence is rather too good to be true. Of course, it is being emphatically stated that the improvisations have taken months to materialize and arose from lengthy debate and problem solving. There is no shame in learning something the hard way especially when it goes against the established norms. Though there were improvizations, the logic of such steps has remained impeccable and looks forward to being vindicated by independent research.

Many issues have been raised and solutions to some have been suggested. Since an integrative view in providing some of the solution was taken, it has created a flexible test which could cater to the needs of social, differential as well as personality psychologists and possibly of test theorists. The solutions are not (as none is) beyond reproach but on theoretical argument and empirical evidence, seem promising. There are many more questions, which remain to be answered. It requires active research from those who are willing to break away from the tradition and look at the same problems differently or even raise completely new questions.

As had been previously mentioned Puhan and his associates, have kept up a steady research approach by developing the equivalent scales of California Psychological Inventory. There are quite a few scales available for research use. Everybody knows the role that funds play in research. Kline has even codified it in his book. The scarcity of research funds as well as the lukewarm reception new ideas get in psychometric research, makes Puhan's efforts that much commendable. These factors should be taken into account when the tendency to criticize the apparent lack of empirical evidences, (as is provided in support of the EPQ) is always there. Apart from the meagre support that one study can provide to Puhan's effort, it warrants the acceptance of the tests that have been developed as research instruments. Those tests were not explicitly developed to generate the Dynamism Indices. But, the possibility of adopting the tests for such purposes is very much there. It appears that the most useful aspect of the PI approach has been that it is flexible. It can very well be used by persons who do not support any of its theoretical basis. It is rather unfortunate that the studies already conducted or being conducted in India did not share the theoretical basis of the current approach that could have unitedly provided a stronger case. Still the lack of such unity at the present moment does not take away the viability of the PI approach at least for the research purposes. Further research will no doubt bring it into the realm of application in many other areas.

It would have been an interesting experience had we been able to replace the stories with short video plays depicting the situations. Tempting though the idea was, with the limited artistic abilities to offer, it was shelved. But that is not to say that someone more gifted than the author will not use it. It is likely to provide (the author has a feeling that it would) better projective stimuli than the verbal description can. Of course, timing of statements and the situation referred to have to be changed accordingly. But such tasks are not so daunting as to stop the progress on such lines.

With this piece of research, the author is not proclaiming that PI is here to replace the traditional methods overnight. There is still a lot of work to be done. But the extensive theoretical analyses provided in of this piece of research will ensure that further studies will not be just for piling up evidence in the fight for a place in the testing methods. It will consist of doing cumulative research by branching and expanding into related areas. Tests like the EPQ have got decades of supportive research. Tests like the PIAPEN lack that kind of empirical support, but have established their existence by correlating with established tests as well as conceptually drawing on such correlations. Further empirical research will reveal its predictive use.

6.2 Bouquets or Brickbats ?

As regards the question of getting bouquets or brickbats, the answer is neither. The evidence provided the indication of the theories and arguments. Kuhn (1970) has talked about traditional sciences providing inelegant and monotonous research because they tend to provide the evidence for something that has already been known by the researcher to be true. But in a science like psychology there are many trifling and unscientific reasons why theory will not be borne out by empirical evidence (Meehl, 1978; Koch, 1981; Fiske, 1979). It is definitely pleasing to see that theory shows some relationship with external world. And yet, had the evidence been otherwise it would not have conclusively proved that the initial theorization were wrong. Any adverse outcome would only have necessitated the writings of better items, greater control of sampling (those elusive gremlins) and further research.

When one uses a lot of argument to support a point, there is always a danger of making a statement that contradicts one's initial statement. Yet, we still relish arguments basically because only through that one can take relatively more correct stand under the circumstances. In this case, there is not much scope left to defend oneself against the lack of evidence. However, all good things come to an end and while the euphoria remains it is only fair to state that the idea of a PI approach is vindicated. The empirical evidence in the form of a test (PIAPEN) is there waiting to be used for further research purposes, opening a whole new vista of theoretical analysis and empirical research.

6.3 Epilogue

It has been a long time since this piece of research was undertaken. Since then, not many studies have been reported contradicting the basic contentions made herein. Not surprisingly, as in Lumsden's case, my arguments have been conveniently overlooked even by Prof. Kline. I came across a book by Kline named *The Emperor's New Clothes* which he was trying to dress psychometrics with. Later, he has come up with a multiply reprinted book *The Handbook of Psychological Testing* in which neither Projective-Inventory nor the criticisms get a mention. Anastasi's newest edition of *Psychological Testing* does not deviate from the beaten track. I find this ostrich like reaction very much antagonistic to real development of understanding of the complexities involved. We need to encourage our students to challenge us instead of subjecting them to our unfolding of half-truths. Lumsden does not get mentioned in Robert M. Thorndike's "Measurement and evaluation is Psychology and Education". Kevin R. Murphy and Charles O. Davidshofer's Psychological Testing mentions Lumsden with reference to some limitations of reliability and true score theory. It does not, however, care to mention that the very concept of reliability as desirable is being challenged. Tom Kubiszym and Gary Borich's "Educational Testing and Measurement" does not mention anything about the criticisms. All these are recent books available in India and currently serve as guides to the understanding of the testing process. This state of affairs has made it imperative that this book be written. Things must change, thinking regarding the concepts must change. And yet, unfortunately, not too many research students are willing to delve deep into the matters and undertake research work in this area. Publication of this may just help in stimulating researchers elsewhere so that the PI approach in its new avatar is put to greater use. What is more significant is the tremendous growth of computer application in the academic sphere, more importantly, the use of multimedia in teaching even at the preschool level. It really augurs well for PI approach as propounded in this study. A short film clip followed by questions would be far more easily accepted than the rather long verbal descriptions resorted to in the stories. The beauty would be in quickly playing back the related clip in a window while the question is being put. It seems like PI is multimedia ready as well as Y2K proof. (For the computer illiterates, help is at hand: Here, the expressions really means nothing). And, for the computer wizards, are you listening?

It is a pity that Dr Puhan and myself could not agree on the point of the impact of social desirability. In his presidential address at the Fifth annual conference of NAOP held at Allahabad, Puhan (1995) has cited a lot of instances of tests developed in the line of Projective Inventory at Utkal. He has also cited many a study shedding light of the vexed problem of social desirability. I, somehow remain unmoved as I am yet to come across studies that counters what I contended in my book. May be after the book, there will be more pointed criticism of the contention so that the approach will benefit more. For the time being, I would back the efficacy of the concepts of Dynamism Indices rather than the efficacy of this approach being SD proof. The wonderful thing is either way the PI approach becomes a more viable alternative.

APPENDICES

Introduction to Appendices

The Appendices contain the original stories (A), the initial statements (B), and the scoring key (C) yielded after item-analysis. When using in one's research, this test can again be used to establish greater universality. It can also be used by selecting those keyed items only and suitably changing their serial numbers. It will be nice if the five-point response scale can be used. A recent study has shown very encouraging results.

Appendix A

The Indian Version of The Piapen: The Initial Test

Introduction

This booklet contains stories made up from real life situations. They are numbered from A to G. Each story involves various characters . They have interacted with each other in their natural way. But reading the stories one can easily have a feeling that things could have been different. Human beings view the same situation differently. There is no "correct" way of seeing things.

Following each of the stories are 30 statements regarding the characters or the situation. You may feel like agreeing or disagreeing with the statements. Circle either "YES or NO" that follows the statements depending on your feelings. Your response will in no way identify you individually . It will help us identify the common response which is the aim of this research. Some of the statements may seem like mere repetition but they deal with different aspects. Please respond as you sincerely agree or disagree with the statements.

There is no necessity of putting your name or signature anywhere. Thank you very much for your kind co-operation.

STORY A

Ram was standing in a queue for a train ticket. He found people jumping the queue. Nobody protested. By the time his turn came, there was no reserve seat left. But he had to go. There was a rush for the seats. He squeezed himself onto a seat in a crowded compartment. One of the passengers tried to start a conversation. Ram did not respond and went on reading a book.

Sometime later, when he looked up, he found a lady standing at a distance and looking at him. She looked very familiar to him. But she turned her face away. Ram hesitated for sometime but then got up and went near her. He asked her whether they had met earlier. She denied Ram lied to her that he would not be travelling very far and told her that she was welcome to take his seat. The lady accepted the offer immediately.

Then Ram went to the toilet. Coming out he looked out of the window. He liked the beautiful scenery and stood there for a long time, alone. Madhabi, the concerned lady, came and thank him. She was to get down at the next stop. The next few minutes were spent in idle talk. Meanwhile Ram had noticed that Madhabi's baggage looked vey much like his own. When the train stopped Ram offered to carry her luggage down. But she politely refused, thanked him and got down.

He stood near the door and looked on. But Madhabi did not turn back to look at him. He felt very upset. As the train started to move out of the station, he went back to his seat and sat down. He wanted to take out the book he was reading. Then he discovered that it was not his baggage. A quick revealed some cheap dresses in it. There was no address or identifying marks. He was carrying a large amount of money in his baggage. He felt so bad he covered his face and wept.

STORY B

Hari involved himself in various activities and had a wide circle of friends. He usually did quite well in his studies. But his parents and close friends always told him that he achieved much less than he was capable of. They advised him to change his ways. But he never could find the classroom teaching interesting. His arguments were not very much appreciated by the teachers. He found himself spending less time on studies than before.

Keshab is one of his classmates. He had a pleasing appearance. He was a good student too. He was purposeful and took his teacher's advice. Most of the time he was studying and preparing for the examination. The teachers and classmates felt that the contest for the first position was in fact to be between Har and Keshab. Hari never liked Keshab's way of life. They hardly interacted with each other.

Keshab stood first, well above Hari, in the examination. Keshab met Hari after the reasults were declared. He appeared to be sorry for Hari. He told Hari that atleast then they should try to be friends as it was the end of their student days. They may never meet again. Hari showed in no interest in Keshab. Some of Hari's friends started criticizing Keshab. Keshab went away quitely. Hari was very disturbed as he did not like what happened. So when those friends invited him to a movie he declined.

While moving around alone, he met one of his teachers. The teacher maintained a distance earlier but behaved in a friendly way and started giving worldly advice. It seemed double talk to Hari and he got fed up. He reacted angrily. The teacher was moved almost to tears when Hari left him. Hari was feeling very depressed. He just wanted to lie down. He got some sleeping tablets, took them and went to bed. In the morning, he was removed to the hospital, unconscious.

STORY C

Usha was the only daughter of very loving parents. Her needs were immediately looked after. But she wanted her own life and respect for her individuality. She would react very strongly if she felt she was not getting her due. People passed strong remarks about her but she simply ignored them. Her brother, however, felt bad when he noticed people's reaction. Her parents decided that marriage was the best solution. They frantically looked for a groom. Usha, unaware of that, planned her future.

She loved Govind, one of her classmates. When they came to know about the parental steps, they just went and got married. She informed her parent but they never came. Govind and Usha's friends helped them. Usha took up a job to finance Govind's studies. Govind completed his studies and took up a job. Usha found herself burdened with household chores. She became irritable and resigned from the job after an argument with employer. Govind did not like it when he came to here of that but did not say anything.

Govind was loving in the conventional sense. He would take her to the movies and give her expensive gifts. She liked them but was never satisfied. She wanted to go back to studies. But she found Govind always trying to talk her out of it with ideas of raising a family etc. Usha spent her spare time visiting friends who seemed to be happy and ever so busy that she felt like an intruder. She stayed home. Whenever she would talk about her feelings to Govind, Govind would show some affection and ask her not to be so sentimental. She felt very lonely in a crowded world. One day, she wrote a note telling Govind not to look for her. She collected the expensive things and walked out of his life.

STORY D

Shyam lived a straightforward life. He either liked or disliked a person. There was no other alternative for him. He would expect the kind of behaviour which he feels to be good from everybody. Once in a student gathering he found a few bullies passing obscene remarks and embarrassing others. Among other ladies present, his friend Seema was also there. He felt that they were too scared to protest. Shyam stepped into the middle and asked the group to stop. They attacked him but Shyam did not withdraw. Some others intervened but Shyam was badly hurt.

When Shyam came back after recovering he was surprised to find that others tried to avoid him. When he talked with Seema, she was as friendly as before, but avoided any reference to the incident. This annoyed Shyam but he did not know what to do.

Some days later, Shyam was travelling in a rickshaw. He saw Seema walking on the road. Shyam stopped the rickshaw and invited her to come with him. She hesitated but as it was raining she came up. During conversation, they realised that they were going to attend the same interview for a job. After that they travelled in silence to the place.

Seema got down first, quickly thanked Shyam and went inside. Shyam paid the rickshaw-driver and followed. In the waiting room they sat away from each other. Seema looked very confident. She went before Shyam. She was smilling when she came back. Then Shyam went in. He felt that the interviewer's questions were irrelevant. He could not answer them. He came out feeling angry. He was unmindful when he crashed against Seema. He said that he was sorry. Seema was not satisfied and stared at him. Shyam ignoring it walked past her. He could feel Seema's angry eyes following him but he walked on.

STORY E

Gopal promised his young nephew a nice toy. But a few days before the nephew's birthday, he found that he had almost no money. He spent a long time trying to find a cheap but nice toy. At last, he found something that he thought would meet the requirement. At that time, a noisy child, no older than his nephew, charged into the shop. When he saw the toy, he snatched it from the counter and requested his mother to buy it for him. His mother scolded him for being ill mannered and ordered him to return the toy and to apologize to Gopal. The child's beaming face became sorrowful. Gopal felt uncomfortable. He pretended that he was not interested and said that the child could have it. The mother did not seem convinced but she paid for the toy and they left.

Gopal then asked the salesman to show other toys. He found none of those like that toy. The salesman, inexperienced and eager, wanted to make some real sales. So he went to other customers offering help. Gopal could not get the service he wanted. He offensively demanded better service. The first salesman kept quiet. Another salesman intervened and asked Gopal to calm down. As Gopal did not calm down, he threatened to throw Gopal out of the shop as he was disturbing other customers. Though others did not say anything Gopal quietened down. The second salesman asked the first to apologize to Gopal. The first salesman was upset and showed no signs of doing so. Gopal swore that he would get even and walked out.

Outside, he stepped on to the road without bothering to look. A car violently braked behind him. Hearing somebody shout he looked sideways. He could see the mother and the child with the toy inside the car. He turned his head and leisurely crossed the road in front of the halted car.

STORY F

Lina's life was carefree and full of excitement. But one day she and her close friend were run over by a motor-cyclist. Her friend died on the spot. She escaped with minor injuries. Angry students stopped the traffic and demonstrated. Newspaper demanded strong action. There is hardly any punishment for such crimes. The judge did not feel like setting an example. The culprit got away almost scot-free.

Lina became withdrawn after that. She started resenting other's presence. Maya, one of Lina's friends, was a social worker. She requested Lina to help her group for a change. Lina always doubted social workers. She thought that they were merely showing superiority over some unfortunates. But she was so depressed that she agreed to try.

They went to help a group of blind persons. Lina was helping Rita who only recently had lost her sight after a road accident. Rita very much resented her fate, and tried to show her independence. Often she got herself into difficulties. This made Lina's task harder. She felt worse because she felt that her friends were enjoying their tasks. In the end, Rita almost grudgingly thanked her but Lina did not care. She was happy that it was over.

She returned to her hostel for dinner. She was hungry but found the food tasteless. The standard of food was a constant source of student grievance but nothing ever changed. Lina over-turned her dinner on the table and shouted. Others went on eating silently. Later, the supervisor came to investigate. Lina invited her to eat the dinner. Before the surprised supervisor could say anything she walked out.

STORY G

Raghu and Kabita were very active students of their class. Kabita was far better in studies. But in other activities they were almost equal. Raghu had started loving her. They worked together often but always in other's presence. Raghu could not express his feelings to her. This created a lot of tension and agony in Raghu.

One day the students, including Raghu and Kabita, went on a picnic in a bus. Only Raghu knew that it was Kabita's birthday. After getting down the students started singing and merry making. But Raghu asked Kabita and they went away for a walk. When alone with her Raghu wished her happy birthday and gave her a present. Kabita, while protesting, accepted it. At that moment they heard somebody singing lewd songs loudly. They turned to find two young men staring at them from a distance. Kabita was furious and wanted Raghu to confront them. Raghu asked her to ignore them and gently led her to a more secluded place.

They sat near a huge stone on top of a hill and spent a long time talking. Raghu noticed the two young men coming uphill. He suddenly pulled Kabita towards him and kissing her declared his love. They drew apart when they heard some remarks. Two other youngsters were going down hill. Kabita demanded that Raghu should do something. One of the young men slipped and rolled a few yards downhill. Raghu rushed to help. The young man was hurt but managed to pick himself up and quietly walked away with his friend. Raghu turned to find Kabita walking away at a distance.

Raghu walked back to where they sat. After a long time, he went back to the main gathering. Kabita was already there. To other's surprise they kept away from each other right till the end of the picnic.

Appendix B

The Initial Statement

STORY A STATEMENTS

1. Ram should have jumped the queue. Yes No
2. People are being very selfish now-a-days. Yes No
3. Reading materials are necessary thing when one travels. Yes No
4. One needs to respond even when a stranger talks to him/her. Yes No
5. Pure aggression can help someone protect the right. Yes No
6. Ram seemed interested only in women. Yes No
7. There was no need for Ram for offer his seat to the lady. Yes No
8. Ram should have immediately acted when he felt that he knew the lady. Yes No
9. If it does not hurt anyone, lying is alright. Yes No
10. Madhabi behaved purposefully to hold Ram's attention. Yes No
11 Ram seemed to be in love with Madhabi. Yes No
12. One should avoid going to the toilet when carrying valuables in the baggages. Yes No
13. The beautiful earth with all its loneliness, is very attractive. Yes No
14. Madhabi's friendliness just before getting down inexplicable Yes No

15. She most likely changed the baggages intentionally. Yes No
16. She should have introduced herself before leaving Yes No
17. It is difficult to believe anybody these days. Yes No
18. Ram's reaction in the end was only to be expected. Yes No
19. Ram should have taken her baggage even when she declined. Yes No
20. It is rather advisable to keep to oneself when travelling. Yes No
21. Madhabi should have declined Ram's offer. Yes No
22. Ladies should avoid showing friendliness to strangers. Yes No
23. Ram could have tried restraining the queue jumpers. Yes No
24. Ram can never forgive Madhabi. Yes No
25. For a small favour, Madhabi was being extra polite. Yes No
26. Ram was ashamed of taking the help of his co-passengers. Yes No
27. One should accept another's show of friendliness. Yes No
28. Talkative persons are generally more helpful. Yes No
29. It is difficult to trust a traveller with a similar piece of baggage. Yes No
30. Weeping quite often lessens the frustration. Yes No

STORY B STATEMENTS

31. For a student it is advisable to have very few hobbies. Yes No
32. Hari should have learnt that helping others meant restricting himself. Yes No
33. The teacher's reaction to Hari's questions were very justified. Yes No
34. Hari's reation to Kesab's friendliness seem right. Yes No

35. Instead of simply walking away Kesab should have reacted strongly. Yes No
36. In academics what matters is who does the best. Yes No
37. Kesab was showing off his success in front of Hari. Yes No
38. Hari's friends could have made him go to the movie. Yes No
39. The teacher should maintain their distance from the students. Yes No
40. Hari was clearly a victim of the circumstances. Yes No
41. Hari was attempting sucide Yes No
42. Hari felt bad because he failed to live up to other's expectation. Yes No
43. Hari did not succeed because the education system is faulty. Yes No
44. The teacher was a hypocrite. Yes No
45. Hari should have been equally blunt with the teacher from the beginning. Yes No
46. When one is upset, friends are the best company. Yes No
47. Hari discovered how hard life has become. Yes No
48. A care-free life is beyond the reach of most persons. Yes No
49. The teacher was wrong in giving unsolicited advice to Hari. Yes No
50. Hari was justifiable very depressed and disturbed. Yes No
51. He was ashamed of facing his parents after the results. Yes No
52. There was a plan to discredit Hari. Yes No
53. The teacher's delayed show off affection was rubbish. Yes No
54. The two classmates could have been friends much earlier. Yes No
55. Hari was jealous of Kesab's achievments. Yes No

56. A feeling of insecurity was always there with Hari. Yes No
57. Everbody should be purposeful in dealing with others. Yes No
58. Appearances count too much these days. Yes No
59. End of the student days are filled with sentiments. Yes No
60. Keshab behaved like a mature person. Yes No

STORY C STATEMENTS

61. Instead of ignoring the remarks Usha should have reacted. Yes No
62. She had all the rights to run her own life. Yes No
63. Her brother was possibly asked to keep an eye on her. Yes No
64. Love of the parent, in the long run, hardly helps anyone. Yes No
65. The parents should have informed Usha about their decision earlier. Yes No
66. A marriage without parent's blessings can hardly be happy. Yes No
67. One can be very lonely in a loving and caring world. Yes No
68. A wider circle of friends generally creates problems. Yes No
69. When in difficulty, it is the friends who help. Yes No
70. Usha should have consulted her husband before she resigned. Yes No
71. Govind was only interested in money. Yes No
72. His advice about personal sacrifice for the family was very sound. Yes No
73. Usha should have reacted strongly to make Govind aware of her feelings. Yes No
74. Women can have their rights by self-sacrifice. Yes No
75. Usha should have gone back to her studies on her own. Yes No

76. She could have talked to her friends about her problems. Yes No
77. The friends she visited must have been really happy. Yes No
78. Usha should have stayed and demanded her full share. Yes No
79. She must have gone to her parent for help. Yes No
80. The note implied that she would take drastic action if pursued. Yes No
81. Once decided to be drastic, one should not compromise. Yes No
82. Changing times is the root cause of all these troubles. Yea No
83. On the whole, Usha gives the impression of being very selfish. Yes No
84. Govind should have declined Usha's offer to finance his studies. Yes No
85. Regard for one's individuality is scarcely useful. Yes No
86. One close friend is preferable to many other friends. Yes No
87. Usha was a helpless victim of the circumstances. Yes No
88. Govind never really loved her. Yes No
89. Marriage should take place after long deliberations and thinking. Yes No
90. Usha will stay away, even if Govind tried his best. Yes No

STORY D STATEMENTS

91. Shyam's strong feelings about right and wrong can seldom be justified. Yes No
92. It is foolish to expect any help from someone these days. Yes No
93. A strong body is essential for survival. Yes No

94. People who talk much in a gathering are usually show-offs. Yes No
95. Shyam should have minded his own business as none else complained. Yes No
96. Shyam should have withdrawn from that place. Yes No
97. Other's reaction to Shyam after the fight was expected. Yes No
98. It was hardly surprising that Shyam's ego was hurt. Yes No
99. Shyam himself was showing off in front of others. Yes No
100. The women onlookers should have supported Shyam. Yes No
101. The students avoided Shyam because they felt ashamed. Yes No
102. Shyam could have asked others about their change in behaviour. Yes No
103. Shyam was very much attracted towards Seema. Yes No
104. Seema was very opportunistic. Yes No
105. It is surprising that Shyam cared to give Seema a lift. Yes No
106. Seema's acceptance of the lift was very misleading. Yes No
107. Conversation between two persons can go on only on limited occassions. Yes No
108. Seema's behaviour became offensive after she got down. Yes No
109. Seema knew that she would get that job. Yes No
110. Job interviews are mostly eye washes. Yes No
111. Shyam reaction in the interview was very much befitting. Yes No
112. Shyam might have deliberately crashed against Seema. Yes No
113. Talking might have softened the situation. Yes No

114. Shyam liked the feeling when Seema stood staring at him angrily. Yes No
115. It is very difficult to be cheerful. Yes No
116. Shyam was unnecessarily thinking too much. Yes No
117. Seema was being unduly aggressive in the end. Yes No
118. Shyam's feeling were changing too quickly. Yes No
119. Seema should have waited for Shyam after she got down. Yes No
120. Seema would have refused the lift if there were no rain. Yes No

STORY E STATEMENTS

121. Gopal was unduly fond of children. Yes No
122. The mother was very harsh on the child. Yes No
123. Learning to say 'No' would have helped Gopal. Yes No
124. Gopal was reminded of his nephew when he saw the child. Yes No
125. The mother left quickly because she knew Gopal's true feelings. Yes No
126. The child should have immedietely returned the toy. Yes No
127. There was nothing for Gopal to feel embarrassed about in the shop. Yes No
128. Lying, as Gopal did, is quite alright. Yes No
129. The salesman should have stopped giving unsolicited help. Yes No
130. It is surprising that Gopal went on looking for that toy for such a long time, Yes No
131. Gopal's annoyance was very much expected. Yes No
132. The second salesman was showing unnecessary bossism. Yes No
133. Asking the first salesman to apologize was really overdoing it. Yes No
134. The first salesman was very nervous. Yes No

135. Gopal's emotion fluctuated rapidly. Yes No
136. Gopal was attaching undue importance to a gift. Yes No
137. Shouting like Gopal did will lead to improved service. Yes No
138. The child's behaviour was very offensive. Yes No
139. Gopal could have tried to put the child more at ease. Yes No
140. Offence was the best form of defence under those circumstances. Yes No
141. The other customers should have intervened. Yes No
142. The first salesman was sure that Gopal had less money. Yes No
143. Some punishment was necessary for the child's stubbornness. Yes No
144. It was really very difficult for Gopal to be care-free. Yes No
145. Gopal could have asked for financial help from someone else. Yes No
146. The first salesman rightly kept quiet. Yes No
147. One has to be extremely careful on the road. Yes No
148. The car driver should have got down and confronted Gopal. Yes No
149. Gopal walked on because he saw the mother and child sitting in the car. Yes No
150. The last act must have satisfied Gopal greatly. Yes No

STORY F STATEMENTS

151. The way Lina lived initially is very difficult to maintain. Yes No
152. The fast vehicles are not appropriate for our social conditions. Yes No
153. The judge was very lenient. Yes No
154. The newspapers most of the times exaggerate the news. Yes No

155. We survive only by sheer chance. Yes No

156. Strong laws are essential for the smooth running of the society. Yes No

157. Lina's change in the life style was only tamporary. Yes No

158. Helping others mostly means showing one's superiority. Yes No

159. Lina could have lessened her depression by mixing more with others. Yes No

160. An unhappy person seldom can be expected to make others happy. Yes No

161. Rita reminded Lina of her dead friend. Yes No

162. There is no point in fighting against one's bad luck. Yes No

163. All other social workers really enjoyed their experiences. Yes No

164. Lina could have exchanged duties with someone else. Yes No

165. Lina rightly expected more gratitude from Rita. Yes No

166. Rita was specifically reacting against Lina. Yes No

167. Very few times complaints produce any results. Yes No

168. The other students silently appreciated Lina's action. Yes No

169. The informer was a wicked person. Yes No

170. Lina's frustrations were bound to be expressed in the described way. Yes No

171. To keep discipline, the in-charge should take strong action against Lina. Yes No

172. There was no possibility of Lina apologising later. Yes No

173. Rita should have accepted her physical limitation. Yes No

174. Maya was not really interested in helping Lina to recover. Yes No

175. Rita will never try doing social work any more. Yes No

176. The in-charge was nervous. Yes No

177. Rita must have made Lina very anxious and unsure. Yes No
178. One can very easily become depressed. Yes No
179. Maya deliberately took Lina to handle the unmanageable Rita. Yes No
180. Rita was worrying more than what was necessary. Yes No

STORY G STATEMENTS

181. To express one's feelings privacy is essential. Yes No
182. Free mixing between men and women is usually bad. Yes No
183. Kabita was in love with Raghu in the beginning. Yes No
184. Picnics are usually very enjoyable. Yes No
185. Raghu should not have gone on a group picnic. Yes No
186. Kabita should have celebrated her birthday at home. Yes No
187. The youngster were just being curious. Yes No
188. Raghu should have faced them in the first instance. Yes No
189. Kabita was being unnecessarily reactive. Yes No
190. Songs can hardly hurt anyone. Yes No
191. Raghu clearly showed an escapist mentality. Yes No
192. It would have been better had Kabita herself confronted the youngsters. Yes No
193. The youngsters must have felt jealous of Raghu. Yes No
194. Raghu's impulsive kissing of Kabita is understandable. Yes No
195. Kabita most likely liked being loved by Raghu. Yes No
196. The other two youngsters were sent by the first two youngsters. Yes No

197. They were waiting silently for Raghu and Kabita to start embracing. Yes No
198. Kabita had strong reasons to feel upset about Raghu's inaction. Yes No
199. Raghu was afraid of what the youngsters might do later. Yes No
200. Raghu rightly rushed to help those youngsters. Yes No
201. Kabita started hating Raghu by the end of the picnic. Yes No
202. A lot of problems can be solved by talking to friends. Yes No
203. The friends should have brought Kabita and Raghu together again. Yes No
204. The two youngsters must have felt very embarrassed at the end. Yes No
205. Hills provide ideal spot for spending time in reflection. Yes No
206. Kabita not returning the gift to Raghu is a surprise. Yes No
207. Raghu should have straight off declared his love to Kabita. Yes No
208. Human love is really very complicated. Yes No
209. Kabita expected Raghu to call her as she walked away. Yes No
210. They should have taken active part in the group merry-making. Yes No

Appendix C

Scoring Key of the Indian Version of PIAPEN

Stories	Item No. (single trait)								Item No. (Multiple trait)	
	PSYCHOTICISM									
A.	4	7	11	12	18	25	27	28	5	
B.	32	34	35	38	40	44	52	55		
C.	61	68	80	87	88					
D.	99	106	109	112	119	120			95	110
E.	130	140	147	150					143	149
F.	153	158	169	174	177	179				
G.	185	186	188	190	191	192	194	196		
	199	203	206	210						
	NEUROTICISM									
A.	5	8	17	29					7	
B.	42	47	51	54	59				40	
C.	64	66	69	70	75	77	86		68	
D.	96	97	101	107	110	113			130	
E.	122	125	127	135	141	146	149			
F.	162	164	168	178						
G.	181	183	187	193	198	201	205		186	195
	EXTRAVERSION									
A.	3	19	21						7	27
B.	45	49	57	58	60				35	
C.	76	81	82	84	90					
D.	95	105							120	
E.	121	143	144	148						
F.	160	170	176							
G.	182	184	195						194	199

Bibliography

Allport, G.W. (1937). *Personality: A Psychological Interpretation*. New York: Holt.

Anastasi, A. (1976). *Psychological Testing*. New York: Macmillan.

_______ (1986). Evolving concept of test validation. *Annual Review of Psychology, 37*, 1-15.

Anastasi, A. & Urbina, S. (1997). *Psychological Testing*. N. J.: Prentice-Hall.

Anderson, N.H. (1968). Likeableness ratings of 555 personality-words. *Journal of Personality and Social Psychology, 9*, 272-279.

Bannister, D. & Bott, M. (1973). Evaluating the Person. On P. Kline (Ed.), *New Approaches in Psychological Measurement*. London: Wiley.

Banu, S. (1981). Further investigation into the Projective Inventory Method. Ph.D. Thesis, Utkal University.

Bell, D. (1972). *The Coming of Post-industrial Society*. New York: Basic Books.

Bell, R. & Lumsden, J. (1980). Test length and validity. *Applied Psychological Measurement, 4*, 165-170.

Bem, D.J. (1983a). Further déjà vu in the search for cross-situational consistency: A reply to Mischel & Peake. *Psychological Review, 90*, 390-393.

Bem, D.J. & Allen, A. (1974). On predicting some of the people some of the time: The search for cross-situational consistencies in behavior. *Psychological Review, 81*, 506-20.

Bem, D.J. & Funder, D.C. (1978). Predicting more of the people Much of the time: Assessment of the personality of situations. *Psychological Review, 85*, 485-501.

Berkowitz, L. (1983). Aversively stimulated aggression. *American Psychologist, 38*, 1135-1144.

Block, J. (1965). The challenge of response sets: Confounding meaning, acquiescence, and social desirability in the MMPI. New York: Appleton-Century-Crofts.

Bock, R.D. & Wood, R. (1971). Test theory. *Annual Review of Psychology*, 22, 193-224.

Bowers, K.S. (1973), Situationism in psychology: An analysis and a critic. *Psychological Review*, *80*, 307-336.

Brogden H.E. & Taylor, E.K. (1950). The dollar criterion-applying the cost-accounting concept to criterion construction. *Personal Psychology*, *3*, 133-154.

Buros, S. K. (Ed.). (1959). V *Mental Measurements Yearbook*. New Jersey: Gryphon Press.

Buros, O.K. (Ed.). (1965). VI *Mental Measurements Yearbook*. New Jersey: Gryphon Press.

_______. (1972). VII *Mental Measurements Yearbook*. New Jersey: Gryphon Press.

_______. (1978). VIII *Mental Measurements Yearbook*. New Jersey: Gryphon Press.

Buss, D.M. & Craik, K.H. (1981). The act frequency analysis of interpersonal dispositions: Aloofness, gregariousness, dominance and submissiveness. *Journal of Personality*, *49*, 175-192.

_______. The act frequency approach to personality. *Psychological Review*, *90*, 105-126.

Campbell, D.T. & Fiske, D.W. (1959). Convergent and discriminant validation by multimethod-multitrait matrix. *Psychological Bulletin*, *56*, 81-105.

Cattell, R.B. and Kline, P. (1977). *The Scientific Analysis of Personality and Motivation*. London: Academic Press.

Cohen, J. (1968). Multiple regression as a general data-analytic system. *Psychological Bulletin*, *70*, 426-443.

_______. (1978). Partialed products are interactions: Partialed powers are curve components. *Psychological Bulletin*, *85*, 858-866.

Coloney, J.C., Kramer, J.J. & Mitchell, J.V. Jr. (Eds.) (1988). *Supplement to the Ninth Mental Measurements Yearbook*, Lincoln, NE : Buros Institute of Mental Measurements.

Coloney, J.C. & Kramer, J.J. (Eds.) (1999). *The Tenth Mental Measurements Yearbook.* Lincon, NE : Buros Institute of Mental Measurements.

Coloney, J.C. & Impara, J.C. (Eds.) (1994) *Supplement to the Eleventh Mental Measurements Yearbook.* Lincoln, Ne : Buros Institute of Mental Mearurement.

_______. (1995) *The Twelth Mental Measurements Yearbook.* Lincoln, NE : Buros Institute of Mental Measurements.

Cooper, C. (1982). *An Experimental Investigation of Freudian Defences.* Unpublished doctoral dissertation, University of Exter.

Cronbach, L.J. (1951). Coefficient alpha and the internal structure of the tests. *Psychometrika, 16*, 297-334.

_______. (1975). Beyond the two discipline of scientific psychology. *American Psychologist, 30*, 116-127.

Cronbach, L.J., Gleser, G.C., Nanda, H., & Rajaratnam, N. (1972). *The Dependability of Behavioural Measurements: Theory of Generalizability for Scores and Profiles.* New York: Wiley.

Cronbach, L.J. & Meehl, P.E. (1955). Construct validity in psychological tests. *Psychological Bulletin, 52*, 281-302.

Crowne, D.P. & Marlowe, D. (1964). *The Approval Motive.* New York: Wiley.

Cureton, E.E. (1939). The principal compulsion of factor analysis. *Harvard Educational Review, 9*, 287-295.

Darley, J.M. & Latane, B. (1968). Bystander intervention in emergencies: Diffusion of responsibility. *Journal of Personality and Social Psychology, 8*, 377-383.

Dawes, R.M.(1979). The robust beauty of improper linear models in decision making. *American Psychologist. 34*, 571-582.

Edwards, A.L. (1953a). The relationship between the judged desirability of a trait and probability that the trait will be endorsed. *Journal of Applied Fsychology, 37*, 90-93.

Edwards, A.L. (1959). *Manual for the Edwards Personality Preference Schedule.* New York: Psychological Corporation.

_______. (1957). *The Social-Desirability Variables in Personality Assessment and Research.* New York: Holt.

_______. (1963). A factor analysis of experimental social desirability. *Journal of Applied Psychology, 47,* 308-316.

_______. (1964b). The assessment of human motives by means of personality scales. In D. Levin (Ed.), *Nebraska Symposium on Motivation.* Lincoln: University of Nebraska Press.

_______.(1969). Trait and evaluative consistency in self-description. *Educational and Psychological Measurement, 29,* 735-752.

_______. (1970). *The Measurement of Personality Traits by Scales and Inventories.* New York: Holt.

Edwards, A.L. & Abbott, R.D. (1973). Measurement of personality traits: Theory and technique. *Annual Review of Psychology, 24,* 241-278.

Epstein, S. (1979). The stability of behavior: On predicting most of the people much of the time. *Journal of Personality and Social Psychology, 37,*1097-1126.

_______. (1983). The stability of confusion: A reply to Mischel and Peake. *Psychological Review, 90,*179-184.

Eysenck, H.J. (1955). Cortical inhibition, figural after-effect and theory of personality. *Journal of Abnormal Social Psychology, 51,*94 -106.

Eysenck, H.J. & Eysenck, S.B.G. (1964). *Manual of the Eysenck Personality Inventory.* London: University of London Press.

_______. (1975). *Manual of the Eysenck Personality Questionnaire.* San Diego, California. EDITS

Fiske, D.W. (1973). Can a personality construct be validated empirically? *Psychological Bulletin, 80,* 89 - 92.

_______. (1974). The limits for a conventional science of personality. *Journal of Personality, 42,* 1-11.

Fiske, D.W. (1976). Can a personality construct have a singular validational pattern? Rejoinder to Huba & Hamilton. *Psychological Bulletin, 83*, 877 - 79.

_______. (1978). *Strategies for Personality Research*. San Fransisco : Jossey - Bass .

_______. (1979). Two Worlds of Psychological Phenomenon. *American Psychologists, 34*, 733 -739.

Fitzpatrick, A.R. (1983). The Meaning of Content Validity. *Applied Psychological Measurement, 7*, 3 - 13

Funder, D.C. (1983). Three Issues in predicting more of the people; a reply to Mischel & Peake. *Psychological Review, 90*, 283 - 289.

Gleser, G.C. (1969). Discussion. Proceedings of the invitational conference on testing problems. Princeton NJ: Educational Testing Service.

Goldberg, L.R. (1972). Some recent trends in personality assessment. *Journal of Personality Assessment, 36*, 547-560.

Green, B.F. (1980). Note on Bem and Funder's scheme for Q Sorts. *Psychological Review, 87*, 212-214.

Hampson, S.E., John, O.P., & Goldberg, L.R. (1986). Category breadth and hierarchical structure in judgement of trait implications. *Journal of Personality and Social Psychology, 51*, 37-54.

Harman, H.H. (1976). *Modern Factor Analysis*. Chicago: University of Chicago Press.

Hartshorne, H. & May, M.A. (1928). *Studies in Deceit*. New York: Macmillan.

_______. (1929). *Studies in Service and Self-control*. New York: Macmillan.

Hashemi, K. (1981). *The Factorial Structure of the Eysenck Personality Questionnaire and the Sixteen Personality Factor Questionnaire*. Ph.D. Thesis, University of Exter.

Helmes, E. (1980). A psychometric investigation of the Eysenck Personality Questionnaire. *Applied Psychological Measurement, 4*,43-55.

Hilgard, E.R. (1980). Consciousness in contemporary psychology, *Annual Review of Psychology,* 1-26.

Hogan, R. (1978). In O.K. Buros (Ed.) *VIII Mental Measurements Year Book,* NJ: Gryphon Press.

Hogan, R., Desoto, C.B. & Solano, C. (1977). Traits, tests and personality research. *American Psychologist, 32*, 255-264.

Holden, R.R. & Jackson. D. N. (1979). Item subtlety and face validity in personality assessment. *Journal of Consulting and Clinical Psychology, 47*, 459-468.

Huba, G,J & Hamilton, D.L. (1976). On the generality of trait relationships: some analyses based on Fiske's paper. *Psychological Bulletin, 83*, 868-876.

Jackson, D.N. (1971b). The dynamics of structured personality tests. *Psychological Review, 78*, 229-248.

_______. (1974). *Personality Research Form Manual.* Port Hurn, Michigan: Research Psychological Press.

Johnson, J.H. Null, J.N. & Johnson, K.N. (1984). Personality processes and individual differences : Replicated item level factor analysis of the full MMPI. *Journal of Personality and Social Psychology,* 105-114.

Jourard, S.M.(1979). *Self-disclosure: An Experimental Analysis of the Transparent Self.* New York: R.E.Krieger.

Kelly, G. (1955). *The Psychology of Personal Constructs.* New York: Noiton.

Kiesler, C. (1982). Comments. In S.M. Clark & S.T. Fiske (Eds.) *Affect and Cognition.* Hillsdale, NJ: Erlbaum.

Kirby, D.M. & Gardner, R.C. (1972). Ethnic stereotypes: Norms on 208 words typically used in their assessment. *Canadian Journal of Psychology, 26*, 140-154.

Kline, P. (1983). *Personality Measurement and Theory.* London: Hutchinson.

_______. (1993). The Handbook of Psychological Testing. London : Routledge.

Kline, P. & Barrett, P. (1983). The factors in personality questionnaires among normal subjects. *Advances in Behaviour Research and Therapy, 5*, 141-202.

Koch, S. (1981). The nature and limits of psychological knowledge : Lessons of a century qua "science". *American Psychologist*, *36*, 257-269.

Kohlberg, L. (1963). The development of children's orientations towards a moral order. *Vita Humana*, 6, 11-33.

_______. (1964). The development of moral character and moral ideology. In M.N. Hoffman & L.W. Hoffman (Ed.) *Review of Child Development Research* (vol.1). New York: Sage Foundation.

_______. (1969). Stage and sequence: The cognitive development approach to socialization. In D.Goslin (Ed.) *Handbook of Socialization Theory and Research*. Chicago: Rand McNalley.

Kubiszyn, T. & Borich, G. (1993). Educational Testing and Measurement. New York : Harper-Collins.

Kuder, G.F. & Richardson, M.W. (1937). The theory of estimation of test reliability. *Psychometrika*, *2*, 151-160.

Kuhn, S. (1970). *The Structure of Scientific Revolutions*. Chicago: University of Chicago Press.

Lamiell, J.T. (1981). Towards an idiothetic psychology of personality. *American Psychologist*, *36*, 276-289.

Lord, F.M. & Novick, F.R. (1968). *Statistical Theory of Mental Test Scores*. Reading: Addison-Wesley.

Lumsden, J. (1961). The Construction of unidimentional tests. *Psychological Bulletin*, *58*, 122-131.

_______. (1976). Test theory. *Annual Review of Psychology*, 27, 251-280.

_______. (1977). Person reliability. *Applied Psychological Measurement*, *1*, 477-482.

_______. (1978). Tests are perfectly reliable. *British Journal of Mathematical and Statistical Psychology*, *31*, 19-26.

Lumsden, J. & Ross, J. (1973). Validity as a theoretical equivalence. *Australian Journal of Psychology*, *25*, 191-197.

Makintosh, N.J. (1974). *The Psychology of Animal Learning*. London: Academic Press.

Mackintosh, N.J. (1983). *Conditioning and Associative Learning*. Oxford: Clarendon Press.

Maddi, S.R. (1980). The uses of theorizing in personology. In E. Staub (Ed.) *Personality: Basic aspects and current research*. Englewoods, N.J.: Prentice-Hall.

Magnusson, D. & Endler, N.S. (Eds.) (1977). *Personality at the Crossroads: Current Issues in Interactional Psychology*. Hillsdale, NJ: Erlbaum.

Mandler, G. (1982). Cognitive underpinnings of affect. In M.S. Clark & S.T. Fiske (Eds.) *Cognition and Affect*. Hillsdale, NJ: Erlbaum.

Maslow, A.H. (1965). Some basic propositions of a growth and self-actualization. In G. Lindzey & C. Hall (Eds.) *Theories of Personality: Primary sources and research*. New York: Wiley.

McClelland, D.C. (1973). Testing for competence rather than for intelligence. *American Psychologist*, 28, 1-14.

Meehl, P.E. (1978). Theoretical risks and tabular asterisks: Sir Kirl, Sir Ronald, and the slow progress of soft psychology. *Journal of Consulting and Clinical Psychology*, 46,807-834.

Meehl, P.E. & Hathaway, S.R. (1946). The K factor as a suppressor variable in the Minnesota Multiphasic Personality Inventory. *Journal of Applied Psychology, 30*, 525-564.

Mischel, W. (1968). *Personality and Assessment*. New York: Wiley.

_______. (1973). Towards a cognitive social learning reconceptualization of personality. *Psychological Review, 4*, 252-283.

_______. (1977). The interaction of person and situation. In D. Magnusson & N.S. Endler (Eds.) *Personality at crossroads: Current issues in interactional psychology*. Hillsdale, NJ: Erlbaum.

_______. (1979). On the interface of cognition and personality Beyond the person-situation debate. *American Psychologist, 34*, 740-754.

Mischel, W. & Peake, P.K. (1982). Beyond déjà vu in cross-situational consistency. *Psychological Review*, *89*, 730-755.

Mischel, W. & Peake, P.K. (1983). Some facts of consistency: Replies to Epstein, Funder, and Bem. *Psychological Review*, *90*, 394-402.

Messick, S. (1975). The standard problem: Meaning and values in measurement and education. *American Psychologist*, *30*, 955-966.

Murphy, K.R. & Davidshofer, C.O. (1998). Pshchological Testing. New Jersey : Prentice-Hall.

Murray, H.A. *et al.* (1938). *Explorations in Personality*. New York: Oxford.

Nunnally, J.C. (1967). *Psychometric Theory*. New York: McGraw-Hill.

_______. (1978). *Psychometric Theory*. New York: McGraw-Hill.

Orne, M.T. (1962). On the social psychology of psychological experiment: With particular reference to demand characteristics and their implications. *American Psychologist*, *17*, 776-83.

Orne, M.T., Thackray, R.I. & Pasketitz, D.A. (1972). On the detection of deception. In N.S Greenfield & R.A. Sternbach (Eds.) *Handbook of Psychophysiology*. New York: Holt.

Patnaik, G. (1988). Contribution of social desirability to Projective Inventory test scores. Unpublished doctoral dissertation, Utkal University.

Puhan, B.N. (1982). *Issues in Psychological Measurement*. Agra: National Psychological Corporation.

_______. (1995) *Projective-Inventory: An indigenous approach to personality assessment*. Presidential address, Fifth NAOP Conference at Allahabad.

Puhan, B.N. & Dash, U.N. (1985). Social desirability components in Projective-inventory based data. *Journal of Social and Economic Studies*, 2, 243-251.

Puhan, B.N. & Rath, P.K. (1981). Projective-Inventory: A new approach to personality assessment. *Asian Journal of Psychology and Education, 7,* 16-24.

Puhan, B.N. & Roy, P. (1985). *Contribution of Social Desirability Factors to Projective-Inventory Scores.* Unpublished Manuscript, Utkal University.

Rappaport, A. (1962). The use and misuse of game theory. *Scientific American, 108,* 108-119.

Rasch, G. (1960). *Probabilistic Models for Some Intelligence and Educational Tests.* Copenhagen: Danish Institute of Educational Research.

Rogers, C.R. (1973). Some new challenges. *American Psychologist, 28,* 379-387.

Rogers, T.B. (1981). A model of the self as an aspect of human information processing system. In N. Cantor & J.F. Kihlstrom (Eds.) *Personality, Cognition, and Social Interaction.* Hillsdale, N.J: Erlbaum.

Rorer, L.G. & Widiger, T.A. (1983). Personality structures and assessment. *Annual Review of Psychology, 34,* 431-63.

Rosenzweig, S. (1945). The Picture-association method and its application in a study of reaction to frustration. *Journal of Personality, 14,* 3-23.

Sandven, J. (1975). *Projectometry.* Oslo: Universitetsforlaget.

Scheibe, K.E. (1979). *Mirrors Masks Lies Secrets: The Limits of Human Predictability.* New York: Praeger.

Stein, K.B. (1970). The TSC scales: Social undesirability or personal adjustment? A reply to Edwards, Klockars & Abbott. *Multivariate Behavioural Research, 5,* 157-158.

Tellegen, A. Kamp, J.& Watson, D. (1982). Recognizing individual differences in predictive structure. *Psychological Review, 89,* 95-105.

Thorndike, R.L. & Hagen, E. (1977). *Measurement and Evaluation in Education and Psychology.* New York: Wiley.

Thorndike, R.M. (1997). Measurement and Evaluation in Psychology and Education. New Jersey : Prentice-Hall.

Tryon, W.W. (1979). The test-trait fallacy. *American Psychologist, 34,* 402-406.

Velicer, W.F. & Stevenson, J.F. (1978). The relation between item format and structure of the Eysenck Personality Inventory. *Applied Psychological Measurement*, 2, 293-304.

Walsh, J.A., Penberthy, D.K. & Earley, S.R. (1969). Relationship between estimated occurrences and social desirability scale value of objective personality items. *American Psychologist*, *24*, 621-622.

Watson, J.B. (1913). Psychology as the behaviorist views it. *Psychological Review*, *20*, 43-77.

Weiner, B. (1982). The emotional consequences of causal attribution. In M.S. Clark & S.T.Fiske (Eds.) *Cognition and Affect*. Hillsdale, NJ: Erlbaum.

Zajonc, R.B. (1980). Feeling and thinking: Preferences need no inferences. *American Psychologist*, *35*, 151-175.

Index

Ability testing, 53
Act-frequency analyses, 25
Activities, 137
Administration, 78, 82, 110, 111
Adults extraversion, 33
Aggression, 91
Allen, A., 22, 27, 28
Allport, G.W., 30
Ambiguities, 110
American Psychological Associations, 88
Anastasi, A., 2, 53, 57, 80, 95, 96, 97, 132
Anderson, N.H., 71
Animal psychology, 12
Anomalies, 100
Anti-SD warfare, 57-58
Assessment, 1, 9
Autonomy, 91

Banu, S., 122
Bayesian revolution, 85
Behavioural construction trategies, 24-25
Behavioural descriptions, 26-28
Behavioural taxomany, 4
Bell, D., 16
Bem, D.J., 22, 27, 28
Berkowitz, L., 63
Better future, 120-24
Block, J., 53
Bock, R.D., 77, 85
Bouquets, 131-32
Bowers, K.S., 19
Brickbats, 131-32
Brogden, H.E., 28
British PIAPEN, 109
British testing, 108
Buros, S.K., 2
Buss, D.M., 25

California psychological inventory, 122, 130
Cattell, R.B., 76
Challenges, 62, 80
Churchillean pipe, 35
Cognitive connotations, 64
Cognitive considerations, 24-25
Cohen, J., 19
Coin tossing, 15
Coloney, J.C., 2
Committing crimes, 54
Computations, 121
Computer gumble, 115
Computer wizards, 133, 39
Conceptualization, 9, 39, 45, 46, 62, 80
Concurrent validity, 88
Conflict resolution test, 4
Consistency, 22, 38-39
    discovery of, 23-24
Constraints, 6, 13, 111
Construct validity, 88, 91, 93
Content validity, 89
Contentions, 29-30
Contradictions, 32
Controversies, 8-10, 11, 12, 67
Cooper, C., 114
Correlation, explanations of, 20-21
    computation of, 117-18
Crime watch program, 68
Criterion validity, 88
Criticisms, 4, 13, 132, 134
Cronbach, L.J., 17, 79, 82, 84, 91
Crossbreeding, 5
Cross-situational consistency, 23
Crowne, D.P., 50
CTBT., 98
Cureton, E.E., 114

Data collections, 109, 112-13
Dawes, R.M., 17
Default options, 115-16
Defomation, 49
Demonstration, 3, 8, 20, 54
    discrepancy, 26
Desirability, components of, 35-36
Deviation I.Q. scores, 43
Dichotomy, 63
Dollar criteria, 28
Double approach avoidance, 37
Dust-bowl empiricism, 101
Dynamic conception, 37
Dynamic resolution, 71
Dynamic traits, 129
Dynamism Indices (DIs), 42-43,45, 95, 98,104,119,121,124,127,129, 130,134

Ecological psychology, 44
Edwards, A.L., 31, 49, 52, 54, 69, 70, 71
forced-choice method, 73
Edwards Personal Preference Schedule (EPPS), 48, 54, 55, 73
Electro megnatic waves, 95
Encoding strategies, 24
Endler, N.S., 22
EPQ, 30, 40, 41, 56, 61, 98, 100, 104, 107, 128
approaches, 116
Epstein, S., 22, 23
Establishing rapport, 59-60
Ethical constraints, 7
Extraversion, 25, 29, 36, 107, 113, 122, 127, 155
Extremism trait, 38
Eysenck, H.J., 10, 29, 56, 58, 60, 66

Face validity, 89-90
Factor identification, 118-19
Fake-proof tests, 58-60
Fight and survival, 52-53
First attempt, 106-108
Fiske, D.W., 91, 102
Fitzpatrick, A.R., 90
Fluctuations, 36, 38, 40, 86-87
Fundamental issues, 8

Gleser, G.C., 90
Goldberg, L.R., 22
Grid approach, 4
Group testing situation, 59

Hamilton, D.L., 91
Hampshire, 26
Hampson, S.E., 39
Harman, H.N., 114
Hartshorne, H., 65
Hashemi, K., 114
Helmer, E., 104
Hilgard, E.R., 62
Hobbies, 112-13
Hogan, R., 10, 57, 76
Huba, G.J., 91

Ideographic approach, 27
Ideosyncratic judgement, 6
Ideothetic measurement, 27
Improvisations, 130
Improper linear model, 19
Inconsistency, 22, 39, 59
Indian Council for Social Science Research (ICSSR), 7
InkBlot test, 6
Intellectual ascendency, 51
Interchangeable measuring instruments, 91
Introversion, 36
Inventories, 2, 56, 105
approach, 3
Item format, 105-106
Item selection, 124-25

Jackson, D.N., 57, 76, 89
Jargons, proliferation of, 101
Johnson, J.H., 25, 115
Jourard, S.M., 50, 65, 66

Kelly, G., 3
Keying, 107, 124
issues of, 125
Kiesler, D.D., 63
Kline, P., 14, 18, 22, 35, 36, 53, 55, 75, 76, 104, 108, 122, 124, 125
Koch, S., 67
KR-20, 80
Kubiszyn, T., 133
Kuder, G.F., 79
Kuder-Richardson formula, 78
Kuhn, S., 97, 131

Lamiell, J.T., 26, 27
Lesser mortals, 35
Lie scores, 56, 107
Loading of markers, 118
Lord, F.M., 84
Low predictive validity, 21
Lumsden, J., 9, 77, 78, 84, 92, 93, 96

Mackintosh, N.J., 12
Maddi, S.R., 25
Magnusson, D., 22
Maladies, 114
Marlowe-Crowne desirability scale, 58
Maslow, A.H., 63
Mathematical rationalisation, 114
McClelland, D.C., 87
Measurement, error of, 80-81
Meehl, P.E., 12, 19, 49, 65, 66, 132
Mental measurement yearbook, 75
Messick, S., 90
Mini Paradigm, 100
Minsk-Pinsk dilemma, 16

Mischel, W., 11, 12, 18, 21-23, 24, 76
Multiple Keying, 103-105, 125
Multiple regression, 19-20
Multitrait-Multimethod approach, 7, 92
Multitrait-Multimethod Matrix (MTMM), 90
Murphy, Kevin R., 6, 131

NATO, 115
Neologisms, 101
Neo-Sheldoman analogy, 36
Neuroticsm, 29, 30, 103, 107, 113, 119, 123, 127, 155
Nomethetic approach, 27, 127
Novick, F.R., 84
Nuclear armaments, 98
Nunnally, J.C., 95, 108
Nutshell, 73

Objective observations, 28
Oedipus complex, 51
Old trichotomy, 30
Operationism, 94
Opposing forces, 30
Optimism, 5
Orne, M.T., 40, 65

Paradigmatic stability, 97
Parsimony, law of, 71-72
Patnaik, G., 7, 122
Pedigree, 46, 111
Personal deviation, 121
Personal Research Form (PRF), 57
Personality arena, 106
  coefficient, 11, 76
  factors, 42, 56
  inventories, 65, 106
  parameters, 59
  psychology, 26
  statement, 47
  testing, 1, 3, 55, 98
Passimism, 108
Picture-frustration test, 4
Piles, 112
Poppycock, 22
Predictability, characterises of, 15-16
Prediction, 15, 18, 20, 102
Predicting behaviour, 13-15
Principal Components Analysis (PCA), 125
Projective Inventory (PI) approach, 5, 23, 100, 102
  contributions of, 41-42
  idea to the test, 100-101
  keying, 102-103
  lookback, 116-117
  method, 9
  preliminary analysis, 115-116
  theoretical bases of, 120
  using factor analysis, 113-114
Projective Inventory Analogue of Psychoticism, Extension and Neuroticism (PIAPEN), 101, 102, 104, 105, 110, 116
  Indian version of, 136-40, 155
Projective techniques, 2, 3, 52
Projective test, 51
Proliferation, 102
Prototype testing, 7
Psychological explanations, 72
Psychological measurement, 65
Psychological test, 60-61,99
Psychological test and diagnostic, technical recommendations for, 88
Psychometrician, 10, 13, 49, 55, 93
  conceptualisation, 27
Psychoticism, 29, 30, 41, 103, 107, 122-23, 124, 127, 155
Public resentment, 62
Pudding taste, 100-120
Puhan, B.N., 4, 5, 7, 9, 122
Punishment, 68

Q-sort techniques, 28

Rappaport, A., 15
Rapport, basic process of, 60
Ross, J., 93
Rath, P.K., 5, 7, 9
Reading test, validity of, 89
Reality, 62-63
Reconceptualization, 9, 22, 29, 68
Rediscovering, 113
Regression equation, 20
Reinforcement contingencies, 33
Reliability, 76-78, 80, 122
  coefficients, 85
  error component of true scores, 83-84
  limitations, 78, 133
  potential utility of, 85
  problems of, 80-87
  test, 86

theoretical issues, 82-85
Richardson, M.W., 79
Rigid conceptualization, 70
Rogers, C.R., 62, 63
Rorer, L.G., 18, 21

Sandven, J., 4
Scale reliability, 106
Scheibe, K.B., 16
Scoring, 113
key, 155
Second attempt, 110
Self-confessions, 67
Self-sincerity, ubiquitous problem of, 67
Shakespeare, 81, 85
Silly questions, 61-62
Single trait keying, 104
Situational tests, 42
Skepticism, 14
Social Desirability (SD), 37, 53, 68-69, 108
connotation, 56
context, 65
dimension, 31, 48
problems, 7
syndrome, 48
Social Desirability Effect (SDE), 7, 8, 9, 46, 125
discovery of, 47-48, 69-70
Social Desirability Scale Value (SDSV), 48, 50, 52, 53, 73, 105
Social exigencies, 66
Social reinforcement, processes of, 34
Socialization, 32-33
Soothsayers, 16
Spearman-Brown prophecy formula, 78
Standard Error of Measurement (SEM), 81, 90
Strait-Jacketing, 36
Susceptibility, 55

Tackling, 58
Taylor, E.K., 28
Technological advancement, 57
Tellegen, A., 28
Test Development Ban Treaty, 98
Teste taking ability, 54
Testing personality, 111, 129
method of, 74, 101
Testing process, platonic conception of, 8
Testing reliability, 40, 75, 78
Testing sessions, 111, 112
Thematic Apperception Test, 6
Thorndike, R.M., 89, 133
Thurstonian simple structure, 29
Traditional inventory approach, 73
Traits, 4, 5, 24, 39, 71, 72, 127
cognitive reconceptualization, 23
conceptualisation, 101-102, 125-26
controversy, 126
defence of, 10-11
demonstration of, 34
fixity of, 36
growth of, 32
indicative behaviour, 26
intra-individual distribution of, 37
measurement, 104
psychology, 25
scores, 107
studies, 28
Trichotomy, 63
Tryon, W.W., 10

Unfathomable organismic factors, 13
University sophomores, 35
Utkal University, 111

Validities, 55, 76, 88-89, 94, 122
formulation of, 88-89
multitrait-multimethod approach, 90-91
objections, 94-95
problems, 55, 95
tests, 75
Varimax rotation, 115
Velicer, W.F., 106
Vulger analogy, 79

Walsh, J.A., 50
Walson, J.B., 12, 13
Weapons control, 128
Weiner, B., 63
Widiger, T.A., 18, 21
Wild fluctuation, 35

Y2K proof, 133

Zajonc, R.B., 63
Zeitgeist, 28